THERE AND BACK
by
CORNELIUS TURNER

First published in 2008
In
Great Britain by
ARIZOWN PRODUCTIONS
84, Berry Hill Road,
MANSFIELD, Notts. NG18 4RR.

Copyright:-
Caroline Farthing and Christopher Turner.

All Rights Reserved.
No part of this publication may be reproduced, stored in a retrieval system, or transmitted in any form, or by means, electronic, mechanical, photocopying, recording or otherwise without the prior permission of the Publishers, nor be otherwise circulated in any form or binding or cover other than in which it is published and without a similar condition being imposed on the subsequent publisher.

Cover photograph and design W. H. Stephenson

ISBN 978-0-9559628-0-6
Printed by
ADLARD Print & Reprographics Limited,
The Old School, The Green, Ruddington, Notts, UK
NG11 6HH

There and Back

Cornelius Turner
1913 – 1989
An Autobiography

FORWARD

I am sure that anyone reading this book will agree that it is like watching a film with one's imagination as the screen. The recall of memories, and their detail are amazing. It is a book full of local, social, industrial, wartime and family history. There is a treasure trove of local and European geography as well as some thrilling escapades of the Glider pilots during the war. It tells how, amongst many more things, a man from the small Derbyshire village of Palterton came to meet Tito.

Harry Stephenson

INDEX

Chapter 1.
Childhood Days.
Chapter 2.
The Smiths and the Turners.
Chapter 3.
Working for a Living
Chapter 4.
Juvenile Delinquent.
Chapter 5.
Leaving Farming Behind – the Army – and Marriage.
Chapter 6.
To North Africa and Sicily – plus Meeting Tito.
Chapter 7.
Invasion of Southern France.
Chapter 8.
Italy, Greece and the end of the War.
Chapter 9.
Home briefly, then off to Palestine.
Chapter 10.
Back to Family Life and Farming Again.
Chapter 11.
Postscript.

**Cornelius
with his "Wings"**

Dear Caroline

It has often crossed my mind that I missed the chance of talking to my grandparents of their early days. The Duke of Wellington was still alive when my grandfather was born, and he always claimed to have seen, in his childhood, the Fleet sailing out of Spithead!
Of course we were much in awe of our elders. To Grandad Turner, the man of property, I rarely spoke unless spoken to; his wife was a kind, gentle woman, a marvellously competent housewife, loved by all, coping with a partner who was a bit of a handful. Grandfather Smith progressed from a boarding-school youth, through a worldwide experience of life, to a penniless old age. He remained a cultivated feckless man with a strong sense not so much of humour as an impish devilment. In his still prosperous middle years he already leaned heavily on his wife; Grandma was a severely practical battleship of a woman, kind to me, but no closer than if I had been a puppy in a corner of the hearth.
What a time of change it has been. When I see snippets of film of the twenties I seem to be looking back into another age. Naturally through rose-coloured glass, I see those Sunday summer afternoons, the hum of bees over green spreading lawns and croquet hoops, the rustle of long taffeta skirts, the smell of old books, old curtains, old threadbare carpets, the cries of young sisters quarrelling over an ancient, maimed, second generation teddy bear. But it was also I, who stole, with some sniffling, ragged village lad, into his tiny cottage home to share a slice of bread and lard and a mug of cocoa,

grateful for the warmth of the black-leaded cooking range, its heat stirring the red bobbles of the plush over-mantle. The proud khaki-clad young man whose photo held pride of place above the hearth was hard to match up with the coal-blackened, shambling figure of the man even now plodding wearily up to the door off the day shift at the pit.

Times written indelibly on my mind, tales told too often and tales half remembered, half forgotten, flitting haphazard as a butterfly through my mind, to be recaptured only by a chance girl's laugh here, a breath of wind over a fresh cut hayfield there, the clip-clop of a horse maybe, memories grasped for an instant and lost in time.

So these can only be bits and pieces stretching back over seventy years, set down in an attempt to give you some sort of feeling of the way it was, how it happened then to me. I hope you find some interest in it and that it's not entirely unreadable, even to a twelve year-old.

Your ever-loving grandfather,
Cornelius Turner
Solihull, 1983.

Chapter 1.
Childhood Days

Just the other day Grace and I were at Palterton for the weekend, and out of curiosity I ventured up the backstairs over the kitchen, where my brother had slept for sixty years until he died three months ago.

On the night of Lady Day 1922, six days after his tenth birthday, twenty after my ninth, we had climbed those stairs together for the first time, with a candle perhaps as a special treat, to light the way in that great strange house, echoing in its emptiness. We had moved, that day, lock stock and barrel from Carr House Farm, a mile away below the hill, and it had surely been the most exciting day of our young lives; no doubt we were too soon asleep from sheer exhaustion to worry about the dark, unfamiliar shadows, the wind singing through fresh trees, and all the creepy whispering voices of those old walls. You must have laid awake yourself, listening to them, when you slept there for the first time, alone at the top of that house, last year.

Not much had changed in all that time. School books laid down all those years ago were in the bookcase still, Palgrave's Golden Treasury, Warner and Martens history and Berchardt's Algebra, fire scorched along the spine; and when I pushed open the door of the adjacent store-room, there lay the family cradle. In the rush and bustle of moving and finding places for everything - anywhere will do 'til we sort ourselves out - up the

FAMILY 1920

Arthur (standing), Beth, Ellen, Corney (aged 7) and George.

back stairs had gone the cradle and fifty years on there it was still. George had only been three, so I suppose it was kept handy in case it was needed again. A simple rectangular box, hooded at one end, on wooden rockers, it was black japanned and decorated with varnished-over cut-outs, Victorian fashions, impossibly corseted young ladies, animals at bay, redcoats on guard, ships in full rig flying before the gale, mighty engines, delicate forget-me-nots. It had already served several generations before us, and we five had each spent most of our first year lying in that box, and tedious hours later rocking it.

And what a day it had been, the day we came to Palterton Hall. We would all be afoot before daybreak. Milk the cows and feed the stock first thing - it was going to be a trying day for them. All done and breakfast over, the half a dozen great shire horses were harnessed up, Smart, Blossom, Violet, Flower and the rest; it would be a long hard day between the shafts of the wagons, drays and carts. Ten rooms there were to be cleared of furniture to be loaded behind the horses, old hard stuffed horse-hair sofas, rush bottom ladder back chairs, kitchen pots and pans, milk buckets, butter churns, brass bedsteads, wash tubs, the grandfather clock that's still ticking away at Auntie Beth's. Cupboards, sideboards, stools and the round mahogany table where I sit at this moment putting these words to paper. There were no carpets, but a variety of home-made mats and pegged rugs. The heavy iron mangle, wash tubs and the pig-killing bench made a cart-load on their own. Over all that Mama presided like a commanding general. But we were outside which was Dadda's province and where we lads, running wild

The Author's Sketch of PALTERTON HALL.

PALTERTON HALL
We moved from CarrFarm to Palterton, Lady Day 1922. Grace and I were married from here, and this is Alan's Birthplace.

for the day could hardly breathe for the excitement of it.

The hens, shut in their roosts overnight, would be slung in sackbags willy-nilly a dozen at a time and thrown into the carts and the piglets likewise - and what a commotion they made of it. And now would come the drive. All this cackling, squealing and shouted orders would have conveyed itself to the livestock, and when the young horses, calves, every man and boy on hand with shouts and sticks, well then up would go their tails, heads down, heels in the air, up and off and away, ho, hey tally-ho across the meadow, through the drive gate and up the road, over the hill and far away! Yells and shouts and waving of arms and racing ahead to turn them here and block a gap there! That would be a day to remember for a lifetime.

Luckily for all concerned, with a mile to go the animals had time to get out of puff, and long before they'd rounded the Dark Corner, raced past the Sally Gap, and reached the village street at the top of the hill, they'd be sampling the flavour of the road-side grass and giving us the chance of getting our own breath back too. The sheep, of course, were well used to driving, and in any case our collie dog Gyp could handle them on her own so long as Dadda walked ahead to show her the way. The cows too soon calmed down but the young beast, bold and spoilt by an hour's freedom in this new exciting world would make pretended rushes at the dog with mock tossing of heads from a safe distance as if to say "Just you wait until my horns grow and then I'll show you!"

All day long, back and forth the procession of animals, wagons, carts, ploughs, mowers, cultivators, harrows, rolls, reapers, tools, harness, ladders, ropes, barrows, mills and engines, root-choppers, cattle-cake mills. chaff-cutters and such would have continued while we lads raced through the house, counting the eighteen rooms, the twenty six windows, the attics and the cellars.

All day too, as the rooms were cleared, my mother would have systematically swept and scrubbed down each one until by evening she could declare the old house clean, bright and respectable for its new tenants, and, turning perhaps for one last look at the room where three of her children had been born, she turned wearily to face a new house and arrived, last of all, and fit to drop, at Palterton. The next morning she'd have said "Get that cradle up the back stairs-it'll do there for now!"....And it's there yet!

I was born at Yew Tree Farm, Heath, two miles away across the valley, where my father had rented 60 acres of Chatsworth land and set up farming with a brand new bride at the age of 25. Three years later they had moved with two baby sons, aged one and two, down to the Carr where I spent the next eight formative years, years that seem from here to have been eternally summer, when Arthur and I roamed the fields and hedgerows, woods and streams in unrestricted freedom.

Carr House Farm, Palterton Carr, lay down in the valley, its 150 acres bordering the eastern banks of the Doe Lea stream.

YEW TREE FARM, HEATH.

Deepdale Farm had the land opposite on the western side. The little river gave its name to the Doe Lea valley. Rising a few miles away in Hardwick Park whose deer had once, no doubt, roamed all this land and given a name to the infant stream, it meandered northwards through the valley. Hereabouts Hardwick Hall and Bolsover Castle stood out on the eastern escarpment, three hundred feet above us and looking out towards the Derbyshire hills, purple along the western horizon. Carr means marsh or fen, and, the land had been gradually drained and enclosed into middling good arable and pasture.

The long, handsome, stone-built, slate-roofed house, surrounded by bits farm buildings was a mile from the village on the hill-top, and reaching up to meet my grandfather Turner's land, at Palterton Elms Farm. Best part of a mile to the north lay the close packed row-houses of the mining village of Carr Vale, where the Great Central railway came through from Lincoln to Chesterfield. Up the middle of the valley the single track of the Midland railway connected the coal mines of Glapwell, Ramcroft, Palterton, Bolsover, Markham and Ireland with the steel-works of Staveley and Chesterfield, and, fifteen miles further north, the steel capital of the world, as we were taught at school, the great City of Sheffield. For, despite its romantic name, it was not for its wild-life that the Doe Lea valley was famed, but for its wealth of coal and iron, and heavy industries, breeding hard men. There was not a railway station in the land but heard the clink and clang of Bolsover wagons in its sidings, our teachers taught us, not an ocean or a continent in the whole wide world that did not bear our steel to its

Stackyard where Beth and I played donkey races with the German Prisoners of War.

TO CARR VALE 1M

FP TO BOLSOVER 12M

SUTTON SCARSDALE 1M

CATTLE YARD

STABLE YARD

BARN

COW SHED

GARDEN

PALTERTON 1M

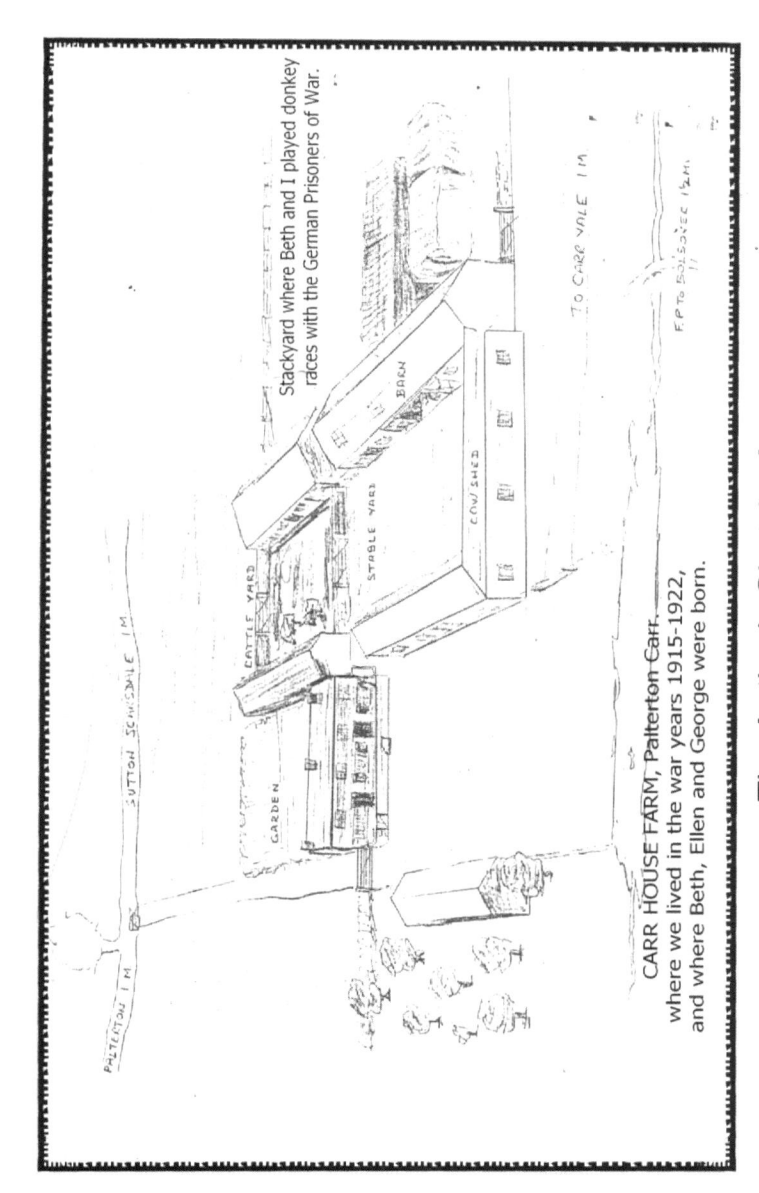

CARR HOUSE FARM, Palterton Carr, where we lived in the war years 1915-1922, and where Beth, Ellen and George were born.

The Author's Sketch of CARR HOUSE FARM.

farthest limits.

We had a pleasant lawn in front of the house where we played our first croquet, and beyond that a sizeable vegetable garden and beyond that again a newly planted apple orchard. A cherry tree and a pear tree grew beside the house and Arthur and I could climb out of our bedroom window onto the leaded flat-top of the parlour bay window and reach out perilously for the fruit in the early mornings before anyone was astir. At the back a stone paved causey stretched the length of the house overlooking the open farmyard, the cattle yard and the pond. At the end of the causey stood the horse trough and pump, our only water supply. There was, of course, no electricity or gas or sewer. Our toilet was a little house beyond the cart-hovel, where a two-seater wooden bench seat covered the dark noisome depths below.

We saw no children to speak to. Men walked the footpaths to and from work in the pits or in family groups on Sundays. We saw no motor cars but enjoyed watching the coal trains and the few passenger trains, and learned to recognise the whistle of the 'Paddy Mail' taking the miners to work and home again. There was no traffic at the farm. Any goods bought or sold we took or fetched ourselves from the station. I suppose this self-sufficiency must for good or ill have had a noticeable effect on our characters.

The milkman called daily with his horse and float to collect the milk - Mr Fullwood, I remember his name now- and he was the only regular visitor. Dr. Saville rode down from Bolsover on his nag now and again, for we had our share of illness. The world beyond the seas was at war but at the Carr we hardly knew it in our own tight little world. We had a man to help Dadda on the farm and a girl in the house. Later in the war we had a girl outside too. She was in the Women's Land Army - Miss Ellis - she was only a slip of a girl, but 'Miss Ellis' she remained until the end of the war, and I never heard her first name. When she left us, we children were quite desolated; she went off to Carr Vale and married a soldier, who had brought a wooden leg back from the trenches of Flanders, and so became Mrs Howarth. We sometimes went to see her in her new home in Charlesworth Street, and a great treat it was as they had a gramophone, the first we had ever heard. We couldn't make out many of the words because most of the songs were by a Scotsman called Harry Lauder whose accent we could not understand, but it was a thrill all the same and magic to us.

One of the men who worked on the farm was Billy Darley whose father had sent him to us to learn about farming, and when he left us they all went to Canada to settle there. And lo and behold, more than twenty years later, in the midst of another war, in walked Billy, now a Master-Sergeant in the Canadian army! Tommy Nuthall was a village boy who was always about the place, one of those lads born to love animals and the land. Then one day we heard that his father Sgt. Nuthall had been killed in France; we never saw Tommy again as he had to go to work at the Pit as the family bread-winner. The war was all about us now. I was in my first year at school and the Headmistress, Miss Varney, put up a poster in the assembly hall of a church in Belgium, its tower topped by the metal figure of an angel; it had been knocked askew by shell-fire, and she urged us with tears in her eyes to bring all our pennies for War Savings to pay back the wicked Germans.

There were some German prisoners of war in a camp at Bolsover Castle and in especially busy times Dadda could ask for some of them to help in the harvest and so on. One day, when we were threshing, we had half a dozen with their funny red and grey sailor hats and odd coloured patches on their uniforms. At lunchtime they had races around the stacks, carrying Beth and I piggy-back, and fell about in the straw laughing and singing. Very jolly men they seemed, quite different from the terrible cruel soldiers Miss Varney had told us about. One dark night there was a sound of distant thunder and we all ran outside to see the searchlights criss-crossing against the clouds. "It's zeppelins over Sheffield" they said in hushed voices as the beams searched back and forth for the great airships, while the thump, thump of the bombs went on and dim flashes of explosions lit the northern horizon.

At last a day came when I was playing, alone down by the pond. Suddenly the blower at the brick-yard began to blow in the middle of the morning. Then the pit blowers from Ramcroft and Glapwell and then Bolsover joined in, and all the pits round about until the whole air vibrated with the whine and whistle of sirens and blowers. I was frightened and ran up the yard calling for my mother " What is it Mamma, what is all that noise?" I shouted. Mother was sitting in the far corner of the sitting room, leaning on her broom, in the middle of the morning cleaning, with the rush bottom dining chairs turned upside -down round the edge of the table. As I came up to her I saw her shoulders were shaking with sobs. I asked her why and she reached out and hugged me to her, "Because your Uncle Tom will never be coming home again - it's the War - the War's over- it's the end of the War," and she buried her face against my shoulder and wept as I had never seen her before and never would again.

That is how I remember 11 a.m. 11th November 1918. Lieut. Thomas Rowland Smith had been shot by a Turkish sniper outside Jerusalem on the road that leads down to Jericho, on 9th December 1917. Thirty years later I stood in the Holy City and read his name, carved there in stone, Lieut. T R Smith, Sherwood Foresters, Btt. Camel Corps. Among the tiny packet of effects that found their way home was a Foresters cap badge and a well used silver banded pipe. I used them both and have them still.

All my father's people were farmers, staid and steady, thrifty and dependable. Hundreds of years of putting one foot before the other in hard labour - that was the war to them, hard labour with oats and wheat and barley, hay-time in the height of summer, harvest in the autumn, always work in the unchanging turn of the seasons. Cattle, sheep and pigs to fatten, milk to sell, cheese and butter to make, eggs to put down, fruit to preserve, unending work to make good all that food sent to the bottom of the seven seas by the German submarines. Hard work, worthy but boring, a dog's life. It would not have done for Mother's folk, a more interesting lot altogether. All her brothers, all five of them, were in the Yeomanry, the Sherwood Rangers, as their father had been before them. The day the war began, 4th August, they'd thrown their caps at the moon and gone! A harum-scarum irresponsible lot! Ben was in East Africa already, but Bert, Sid, Tom and Willie rode off up Tibshelf High Street, four abreast, the Lords of Creation, but for poor Tom so they rode back four years later by way of Gallipoli, Egypt, France, Palestine and Turkey.

Bert had been thirty when the war began, but he was enlisting again twenty-five years later and broke his health in that terrible winter before Dunkirk. But I never heard a word of regret, not from any of them. Hours I've sat listening to their stories, filling them out in my own mind with the shot and shell of battle and dreams of far-away shores. To me they were wonderful men and times many have I leaned back in my chair gazing at Bert's old short magazine Lee Enfield hanging on the meat hooks on the kitchen ceiling, or Sid's Turkish sword, star and crescent on its black hilt hanging beside the fireplace. Not one of them lived to be seventy, or made a penny or left a bean! Except for Willie of course, he's still going strong at eighty-five - there's only him and Mother left. He's had three wives, two of them churched, and they say he's looking out for a fourth, but his greatest love is still to find a listener to his stories of those far-off days of youth.

The men were coming home. The battlefields of France and Belgium had been the scene of four years if unimagined privation and mutual slaughter directed on both sides by generals and politicians to whom uniformed men were cannon-fodder. I suppose young people now will find their history more concerned with our war, my war, 1939 to 1946. They should remember that no experience of the fighting men then was comparable in any degree to the horror of the Great War, and yet, hundreds of thousands of recruits then had already lived all their lives in hard times; many of them were hard men who had been working like slaves in the indescribable filth of the coal-face and sweat of the steel furnaces, and so, for some, the war had had another face. It had taken them into an irresponsible vigorous male society where family cares, and finding work, and the hardships of hard manual labour were lifted from their shoulders. Their minds had been broadened vastly by the sight of a wider world than the mean little streets of industrial England. They were ready to ask questions of their betters.

As their fathers and elder brothers came home, Miss Varney would stand those boys and girls up in front of the school at assembly that day, holding little paper Union Jacks, and the whole school would give them three cheers. I felt a touch of envy that I should never have the chance of standing out there; and if I sometimes stood in the doorway of the house of one or other of my friends, my eyes always turned to the framed photographs of proud stern soldiers that held the place of honour over the dresser. They were scarcely recognisable in the weary bowed, coal blackened men who trudged up the path off the day shift.

I enjoyed school; I could already count and read well before I was five as I had been a frail child, desperately ill for three months with diphtheria around my fourth birthday: I had been spoilt with books and allowed to stay indoors with a pencil and paper. So when Arthur and I presented ourselves at the gates of New Bolsover Infants School at Easter 1918 I already had a good start on most of the rest. From the first I was competitive in my lessons, perhaps as compensation for being the smallest boy in the class. I had had ring worm and lost all my hair and wore a little round skull cap, so my teacher one day said I should be King Canute and seated me in an armchair in the playground while some of the bigger boys swept the rain pools over my feet with the caretaker's broom. I liked the mental arithmetic and spelling tests with which we often finished the day, and in which I could be rewarded by being allowed home ten minutes early. Nine till twelve. one thirty till four were the hours, very strictly kept; lateness meant the cane as a matter of course and no-one left their seats until Miss Varney's bell rang dead on the hour at tea-time. As Arthur and I raced each other home over the fields and muddy footpaths it would be quite dark when we reached home in winter. Miss Mason, the standard one teacher often passed us on her creaking bicycle along the path as she lived with her parents at Deepdale Farm, our neighbours across the valley, half a mile away on the road to Sutton Scarsdale.

Great Aunt Eliza Tempest, who lived with us, had a large jigsaw puzzle map of Ireland which I had done over and over again until I could quickly place Dublin and Cork, Londonderry and Belfast, and I began to see these names again in the Daily Mail under pictures of khaki-clad, steel-helmeted soldiers in a new war in Ireland. There were maps too, in the paper, of a place called the Near East where the Turks lived, and I learned to spell Constantinople, boasting at school that I knew the longest word in the English language. Aunt Eliza was very interested in missionary work and used to have exciting pictures in the post of Chinese coolies with saucer hats and long poles over their shoulders with bundles at each end, and others pulling rickshaws, and of a place called the Solomon Islands where smiling black women gathered bananas in the fields. She also taught me five finger exercises on the piano and sometimes let me use her paints which were hard, coloured tiles the size of dominoes which you rubbed round and round on a plate with a drop of water until you had lovely delicate colours. These tiles were stamped in relief with fat little men and fiery dragons - I'm sure they were Chinese and would be quite valuable now.

As we lived in an area where nine wage packets out of ten came from coal, it dominated our lives in a degree difficult for an outsider to understand. It has always been like that in the coal-fields and remains so today. But it was more so then. All men went to work in filthy clothes, York straps below their trouser knees, water Dixie's slung over their backs, and came home coated and streaked with coal dust to be bathed by their wives and mothers in tin galvanised baths before the living room fire. Skin blemishes and small wounds on hands, faces and shoulders absorbed the coal-dust and healed over, trapping it for life and branding them as pit-men. In those days, when I was still in the 'Infants' there had been work for all for many years, right through the war and as long again when it was over, so the people were not poor. But families were often large and there was little money to spare. They set themselves modest standards; comforts were precious and luxury just a word. Hardly any of the children had seen the sea, nor would they until they'd left school and started earning money for themselves. There were excursions on the railway to Skegness, eighty miles away for 25 pence in today's money and children half price, return fare, but very few of the miners' families went.

Practically all the boys wore short trousers until they left school at fourteen, a very few of the older ones sticking to the Edwardian fashion of knee-breeches. They were topped by woollen jerseys or 'ganseys', often ragged out at the elbows among the rag-tag element, and out at the breeches behind too. Boys wore boots, often replaced by plimsolls in summer. The girls too wore button-up ankle boots and pinafores over their frocks which were usually home-made. None of the women had ever had their hair cut, and Beth and Ellen were in a small minority, among the girls, with their bobbed hair. Clothes grew more ragged as the Coal Strike of 1921 cut into the wage-packets but I never saw country children going bare-foot even in the worst of times. In the mid twenties I saw many bare foot in Nottingham as they doubtless were in other cities where roads and pavements were paved and smooth, but they would have been impossible on our rough untarred roads. There's another factor too. There's a pride among poor folk in the country that falls easily away in the towns; now-a-days people are falling over each other to claim to be in some class called the poverty level. That would have been deeply shocking among the miners then. During the strike I envied most of the other children as they had a daily free meal at the soup kitchen in the Miners Institute Hall. When they brought sandwiches to school for lunch a favourite variety was bread and lard, generously sprinkled with sugar. When I compared this favourably with our bread and home-made butter and cold beef sandwiches I not unnaturally got my ears boxed. Eight hours' work, eight hours' pay, eight hours sleep and eight bob a day was the slogan of the strikers, but I didn't think they ever got it, and after much hardship they went back to work for no more than they'd had at the start.

Besides miners there were of course shopkeepers and journeymen tradesmen such as bricklayers, plumbers, painters, carpenters and joiners, railwaymen, school teachers, farmers and innkeepers; district nurses were beginning to appear to replace the local street mid-wives. No-one could expect work in these journeyman trades without a proper apprenticeship lasting five or seven years, and this applied even in shops such as grocers, butchers, footwear, outfitters and hair-dressers. When this latter trade boomed in the later, so-called roaring twenties, with bobbed hair and Eton crops all the rage, girls were expected to pay a premium for their apprenticeships, as much as £100, two years wages. There were hardly any private cars and more blacksmiths and shoeing smiths than mechanics. These latter were mostly Army taught and nearly all the road traffic that was not horse-drawn was the lumbering solid tyred Army-surplus ex war-time lorries.

Grandad Turner's Ford 'tin Lizzie' was the only car in Palterton. It had an angular shining brass bonnet and heavy brass headlamps. I think he had bought it in 1917 for around £150. Mother took Beth and Ellen to the sea at Skegness for a week in the summer of 1920, Dadda staying at home to look after the farm and Arthur and I stayed the week with Grandma at The Elms. It was a great adventure when Saturday came as we were to fetch them home in the motor-car; the sun was scarcely up as Grandad and Grandma, Dadda, Arthur and I packed ourselves into the open four-seater, and for hour after hour chuntered along the eighty miles of road to the sea. Past the soaring towers of Lincoln, alongside the dykes, seeing our first aeroplane, there on the ground beside the road, looking like a glorified box-kite, we came to a standstill eventually right outside the lodgings in Drummond Road. And after an hour or so, the eight of us packed ourselves once more aboard with the luggage strapped behind and made for home. And home we arrived in the eye of the setting sun without any trouble. You'll have seen lots of 'tin lizzies' on the old comic films and you'll agree that 160 miles in the day with a load like that was pretty good. By 1922 when they had got a bit more plain, having lost their smart brass-work, they were selling at £125, and suddenly motor-cars were commonplace. Dr Saville, who had ridden down from Bolsover on horse-back when I had diphtheria during the War, now had a smart American Star motor-car while Dr Stratton had a gleaming massive De Dion Bouton as big as a Rolls-Royce. But the butchers and bakers were still peddling their wares in high-wheeled horse-drawn vans. The butchers would compete with the farmers and with each other to race the bus the seven miles to Mansfield cattle-market on Monday mornings. Coal was delivered in carts with heavy horses, shot-up in the road, a ton at a time in front of the house. Since every miner got a ton of coal each month free of charge, these heaps of coal were a permanent sight along the rows of terraced cottages. And on the dark hours the carts performed that other essential function of removing the night-soil from the universal earth-closets.

The move to Palterton was bound to make a big change in our lives. Living in a village, for the first time, we had other children to play with, new boys who knew the lore of bird-nesting, the trees that could be climbed, secret tracks through new woods and new kinds of mischief we hadn't picked up on our own. I believe this was probably where my life began to take a different course from my elder brother's; we had been inseparable, often taken for twins, but I was always a little in his shadow, because of the year's difference in our ages. Now more and more the farm became the centre of his existence and he rarely left its confines; even at school he preferred his own company. As for me it was something stimulating to have outside friends especially those I could boss about in a gang of my own. There were, I suppose, seventy houses in the village and I soon put a name to every one.

There were six largish farms and two smallholdings, three shops, two pubs, the Smithy and the Infant's school. No electricity or gas, no sewerage, no bathrooms, no telephones but the one at the Post Office. Many of the older cottages were stone built like the farms they had been designed to serve, dating back to the seventeenth century. The rest were brick, plain two-up and two-down; built and named in rows, the Ten Row, the Thirteen Row from the number of houses, the Dry Bread and Herring Row, supposedly after the mean diet the builder had fed to his brickies for their midday snap, the Transvaal Row with echoes of the war in South Africa. These later houses had been built to serve the pits, opened up from 1860 to 1900, and the pits were on every side. Within six miles you could see at night the lights of Glapwell and Pleasley, Stanton Hill, Teversal, Tibshelf and Pilsley, Heath and Grassmoor, Ramcroft and Palterton, Bolsover, Markham, Ireland and Staveley, Oxcroft, Creswell, Langwith and Shirebrook, pit headstocks every mile. Some of these were great mines employing 2000 men and more, working 24 hours a day, never at rest. There were four or five seams at different levels and the 'cages' at Bolsover were stopping at the Tophard seam, then the Waterloo, the Blackshale, Low Main and the Deep-soft on their thousand yard plunge to the pit bottom. Each seam has its own properties of brightness, hardness or size, all governing its market for house coal, railways, shipping, industrial furnaces, coking and so on. Years later at

East Grinstead, on the Bexhill Line, we saw an old advert of a Hastings coal-merchant – "Bolsover London Brights 39/- shillings a ton, Tibshelf Kitchen nuts 31/6, prices deliveries, at a penny per ton per mile!"

More than half of these pits are now no more. Many of the huge black slag heaps that scarred our countryside have been graded over and re-seeded and you'd never know there was ever a pit there. The footpaths that criss-crossed the landscape from village to pit are disappearing from disuse as no-one walks to work now, what with closures, and road transport everywhere, taking the folk to new jobs on neighbouring towns and cities they would rarely have seen in the early years of the century.

There were 450 people in Palterton, 200 of them children, that is to say under 14, and therefore still at school. After 14 you were no longer a child but a prospective contributor to the family budget. Families were large, half a dozen of them with getting on for ten apiece. There were 16 of the Clayworths under 21, Harold, the oldest, keeping goal for the village team while the latest was still pram-bound. Strangely enough there was no unemployment among the young – perhaps it was the very low wages that guaranteed any miner's son a job at the pit, and the girls went into shops or out into service.

All the games we played that came round from season to season have long ago disappeared. Marbles, whips and tops, shuttlecocks and battledores, skipping ropes, iron hoops that went everywhere with us. I remember going up from the Carr to collect my very first one from George Whitworth the blacksmith one Saturday and how it ran away as we came to the crest of the hill, leaping down the hill, over the hedge and disappeared down our winter sledge-run, and what a relief it was to find it hours later. Bird nesting in season was a universal pastime. There was great respect for property and very little trespassing but bird-nesting in the spring and mushrooming in autumn were winked at. From the village lads we learned all the common eggs and where to find and recognise the nests, often before the eggs were laid. We made our collections in used chocolate boxes, labelled and cotton wool lined. Wrens, blackies, throstles, spinks, green linnets and yellowhammers, stormcocks and starnels, magpies, jackdaws, corncrakes sparrows and redbreasts, skylarks, plovers and woodpigeons besides the forbidden partridges and pheasants, we knew them all, collecting and swapping the eggs with enthusiasm. In the early Twenties, the tobacco companies began to issue cigarette cards again which had been interrupted by the War. Boys weekly tuppenny bloods, also gave away excellent quality 'photos of footballers and cricketers. Everybody collected them. Being 600 feet above sea level, we had plenty of snow in winter and some grand toboggan runs; some of our sledges could go over half-a-mile past the Sally Gap, faster than a car sometimes. Arthur always had the best sledge in the village, or rode it with the strongest nerve, he always went furthest and fastest. He would never accept second place in anything that wanted strength of will, though he was not a ball-player and never took part in team games.

When we got up to the village, Beth, coming up to seven and Ellen just over five went to the village infants' school. The older children went to Scarcliffe or Bolsover. Beth was even then taking a keen interest in books and excelling at school; she was the sweetest tempered of us all, cleanest and tidiest. Ellen was the noisiest and dirtiest. Variously known in the family as the Besom, Sluthermuck or Ripstitch, she loved the outdoors with only a passing interest in school. She was shorter, fatter with rather more striking good looks than her sister. Beth says there were ninety children at Palterton School and there'd be rather more than that going to Bolsover or Scarcliffe. People who hope to end all wars sometimes forget all the fighting that has gone on over the years between street and street and between village and village. With us, fighting between the village factions was common; half-way to Scarcliffe there are two ash trees beside the road, half-a-dozen rods apart and there after school was the venue of the inter-village fights. Each village faced each other in line with their tree while the gladiators went about their business between; it was called the Battlefield even in my father's day.

There were three senior schools at Bolsover, the Colliery School below the hill, the National Church School near the castle and Welbeck Road Council School, each with upwards of three hundred children. My last year at the Carr was spent at the Colliery School. At work or play, year in year out it overshadowed the others; Mr Haddock, the Headmaster was a leading local sportsman and the finest scholarship crammer in the County. Each of his three sons in turn became football and cricket star players at the Grammar School at Chesterfield, Stuart, my contemporary, being Captain of soccer and cricket. I should be surprised if the shouts of "Come on Finney" are not still ringing out somewhere up there. He also remains in my memory painfully; for throwing stones and hitting one of the girls, he gave me four strokes of the cane, a harsh punishment for a little eight year old. A stitch in time perhaps – at any rate I was never caned again throughout my school-life.

While I was at Bolsover School I spent summer evenings and August holidays roaming around the village or about the farm with a gang of guttersnipes recruited out of the rows. If our parents were out visiting we sometimes had high times around the sheds and among the stacks. It only took seconds for them to disappear over the walls if we heard the clip-clop of the horse and trap along the lane, coming home earlier than expected, and we were not surprised if Dadda laid about us with his belt if we'd scattered the hay and straw about the yard making slides from the top of the stacks. In the woods we climbed the trees, and cowboys and Indians stalked each other endlessly. There was a penny film show at the picture palace at Bolsover on Saturday afternoons and whatever the weather I never missed my weekly ration of Douglas Fairbanks, Mary Pickford, Pearl White, Tom Mix and Charlie Chaplin.

At lunchtime on schooldays we explored every nook and alleyway of the little town. Bolsover, with its 12,000 or so inhabitants was the schooling and shopping centre for a number of surrounding colliery villages. Children were not allowed without grown-ups in the Castle grounds, but there was plenty of excitement to be found in the castle fields below the walls, where we could lay along the course of the stream that tumbled down beneath the walls towards the smoke of the great colliery, where it flowed into the Doe Lea, that joined the Rother that joined the Don, that joined the Humber, that joined the sea. I was keen on geography which I still think was well taught then. At nine we learned the features and trades of our town, the whole class joining in making a collage map of the town. At ten we did the county, at eleven – England, at twelve – Europe and at thirteen the World. Like parrots, perhaps, we chanted in unison the names of the rivers, the coal-fields, the cotton and woollen towns, steel and shipbuilding, sea-ports, fishing ports, potteries, the fertile valleys of York, the Trent, the Severn, the Ouse, the wheat plains of Lincoln, the Fens and East Anglia. Simple but effective – but back to play. We hid behind the earthworks that had sheltered the King's men from Cromwell's Ironsides, and scurried in and around the ancient Civil War watch towers that faced over from the western ramparts to the purple wall of the faraway Pennines.

In the playground there was football, fifty-a-side, or cricket with a hand carved bat and, if we were lucky, one of the newly invented unburstable sponge-rubber balls. We had our local heroes and when our own Stanley Worthington scored a century for England, we stood agape as he walked down the street for all the world like any ordinary man. There's a painter, Dutch I think, called Breughel, from Shakespeare's day, which has a painting of a village square packed with children playing all the games of the time. They were nearly all familiar to us, marble, hoops, skipping, wrestling, conkers, letting, whips and tops and so on, nearly all forgotten now.

Peggy was another favourite team game though too dangerous for school playgrounds. You tipped a bobbin into the air from a little see-saw of sticks, and then struck it with a short handy stave before it fell to the ground. If you failed to hit it or if the other side, fielding-out, caught it, you were out. If you hit it, you challenged the opposition to giant-stride the distance in a declared number of strides. If they succeeded they scored the strides, if they failed, you did. This was quite popular with the younger pit-men, as it cost nothing and could be quite as exciting as cricket. It must be nearly sixty years since I saw it played.

Any old pram-chassis was in demand to convert into a shoggey with an old soap box to go racing down our steep lanes until we turned head over heels into the ditch. We used the carpenters shop to carve ourselves wooden swords and guns. Ash grew well in our limestone soil to make bows with hazel wand arrows. There was no shortage of feathers for the Indians as lots of the villagers kept hens. It's strange to realise that in nearly twenty years here in Solihull, I have never heard a cock-crow.

When we were at a loose end, the village smithy was always there. George Whitworth the leather-apronned blacksmith worked quietly and tirelessly through his long days, shoeing horses, sharpening harrows, repairing farm implements, fashioning gate hooks and hinges – he would turn his hand to anything to do with iron. We would edge nearer and nearer the open door, dodging inside and jumping back again as the great horses shot sparks off the stone sets, turning their heads, white-eyed, to the back of the gently murmuring blacksmith. A big lad could take a turn with the bellows while I would watch the hammer clanging down on the anvil, angling and twisting the metal, wondering why the red hot iron was sometimes doused in the water trough and at others allowed to cool naturally. It's always fascinating to watch the rough hands of a craftsman transforming the raw materials of his craft.

Another was Old Jack. Until he got too old for ladders he did the thatching of the corn and hay stacks. One day as he sat on the straw eating his morning snap I watched him twist a couple of straws in a few moments into a corn-dolly. He showed me the trick and I practised it until I could make a passable job. Later, when I worked the horses, I never turned them out without one of these pleated into its tail. Old Jack also did the hedge-laying; you don't see it done much nowadays as forty yards would be a long day's work even for an expert. But well-done, like dry-walling, it is a thing to see that anyone can enjoy looking at.

Old Jack was to be distinguished from Long Jack – a beanpole of a man. He was the village poacher and I never heard of him doing a day's work, but no rabbit crossed the road but Long

Jack didn't pick it up. He used to retire to the work-house now and again but he would be out in time with the daffodil. Now I must move on to school again.

Gaffer Day at Welbeck Road was Bolsover's chief citizen, a magistrate, Chairman of the Council, and generally a figure of consequence. Well over 6 feet tall, thin as a reed, straight as a ram-rod, eyes of palest blue gleaming under bushy beetle brows, his stately measured walk to school, walking stick tucked round his elbow silenced every voice, brought every hand out of our trouser pockets, and struck terror in the hearts of all wrong-doers and even those who were only thinking of doing wrong. He was a martinet with a powerful arm, a bitter tongue and not a spark of humour. His cane was never spared and no parents ever questioned his punishments. Mind you there were some hard cases among those miners lads, but I really believe some of the worst of them were secretly proud of the harshest Headmaster for miles around. He was a gifted man with four ears and an eye in the back of his head! The school was an H-block, its six classrooms each holding thirty two-seater desks; of the six teachers, less than half were college trained but all were very good with sixty pupils apiece. I suppose they were almost as much in fear of the "Gaffer" as we were but always certain of his towering strength behind them.

Nine till twelve, one thirty till four, winter and summer alike. At lunchtime we had sandwiches, eaten in the playground, locked out of school. Although there were buses between home and school it never entered our heads to get on one at a penny-ha'penny the journey, none of us. We walked to school, helping ourselves to raw turnips and greens on the way and raced each other home across the fields at night. There were no free periods. Each day started with assembly, prayers and a hymn. Heads were counted and deliberately chalked up by the Gaffer on the board behind his desk. Total pupils 334. Pupils present 332. Those missing were accounted for with notes, truancy was very unusual and harshly punished. First period Scripture to 9-30, learning hymns, the Creed, the 23rd Psalm and Magnificat, the Ten Commandments and the Sermon on the Mount – "Fifth chapter of St Matthew, beginning at the first verse" we chanted in uniform "And when he was set his disciples came unto him and he taught them saying, Blessed are they........". Arithmetic followed until playtime at quarter to eleven every day. Then two periods until twelve and four in the afternoon. Reading, writing grammar, composition, history and geography, with drawing once a week for the boys, drawing on pastel, and sewing and knitting for the girls. "In, over, through and off!" the unison of knitting came through the screens as we toiled, tongues lolling over our drawing paper. Tables up to twelve times were known by all by the age of twelve and spelling tests and mental arithmetic were used at the end of the day to give the monitors time to clear away the books and collect the pens. At the Colliery School we had used only slates and slate-pencils, but I soon got to use pen and ink.

About four of us were top of the class at various times but when the County Minor Scholarship came around I was the only successful candidate out of the forty who attended in March 1924. And so, in July 1924, I left Welbeck Road; they had done well by me. It was the end of my first six years, full of discovery and easy-going. It was to be the start of my last six years which were to be quite different, in which I had to do the hardest work of my life, and grew to long for the day my school life should be over.

We hear on all sides that more should be spent on education but I really believe that the 1924 elementary schools were very good, and in scholastic level better than most of that age today. At the average age of 11, only one boy in our class could not read out of 60. Our teachers were mostly pupil-teacher trained, starting in the class-room at sixteen or seventeen, working their first year as class assistant, gradually taking on more work until they were fully capable of teaching every subject and accustomed to maintaining discipline. By this age they had taught us our tables, stories of Julius Caesar, King Alfred and the Danes, William the Conqueror and the Princes in the Tower, King Henry chopping off the head of his six wives and Queen Elizabeth defeating the Great Armada. We knew all the coal-fields by name, that the biggest was the York Derby and Notts., the most famous and important pit in all the land was Bolsover.

We had learned the rivers and sea-ports, that cotton goods came from Lancashire and woollens from Yorkshire, that steel came from Staveley, Clay Cross, Stanton and Sheffield and the Black Country where the smoke was so dense you could not see a hand before your face! Lace was from Nottingham, carpets from Kidderminster and pots from Stoke. Railway engines and Rolls-Royce cars came from Derby and the King and Queen from Windsor Castle. The Unknown Warrior was buried in Westminster Abbey. We waved flags on Armistice Day and Empire Day 24th May, when the 'Gaffer' would read out some poetry at Assembly and we'd all rush home at noon for a half-holiday. Who knows about Armistice Day now; for us Bonnie Prince Charlie lived again once a year perched in his oak-tree and for some reason we always celebrated it by chasing the girls with stinging nettles on the 29th May. And so my happiest schooldays, spent in cold class-rooms from which we never moved except at break-times, crowded, often with ragged, smelly, flea-ridden companions came to an end. But before I turn to my Grammar School days perhaps we could leave those coming cares for a moment and turn to the very last bit of my real childhood, the holidays I nearly always spent at Grandad and Grandma Smith's at Tibshelf at Rock House.

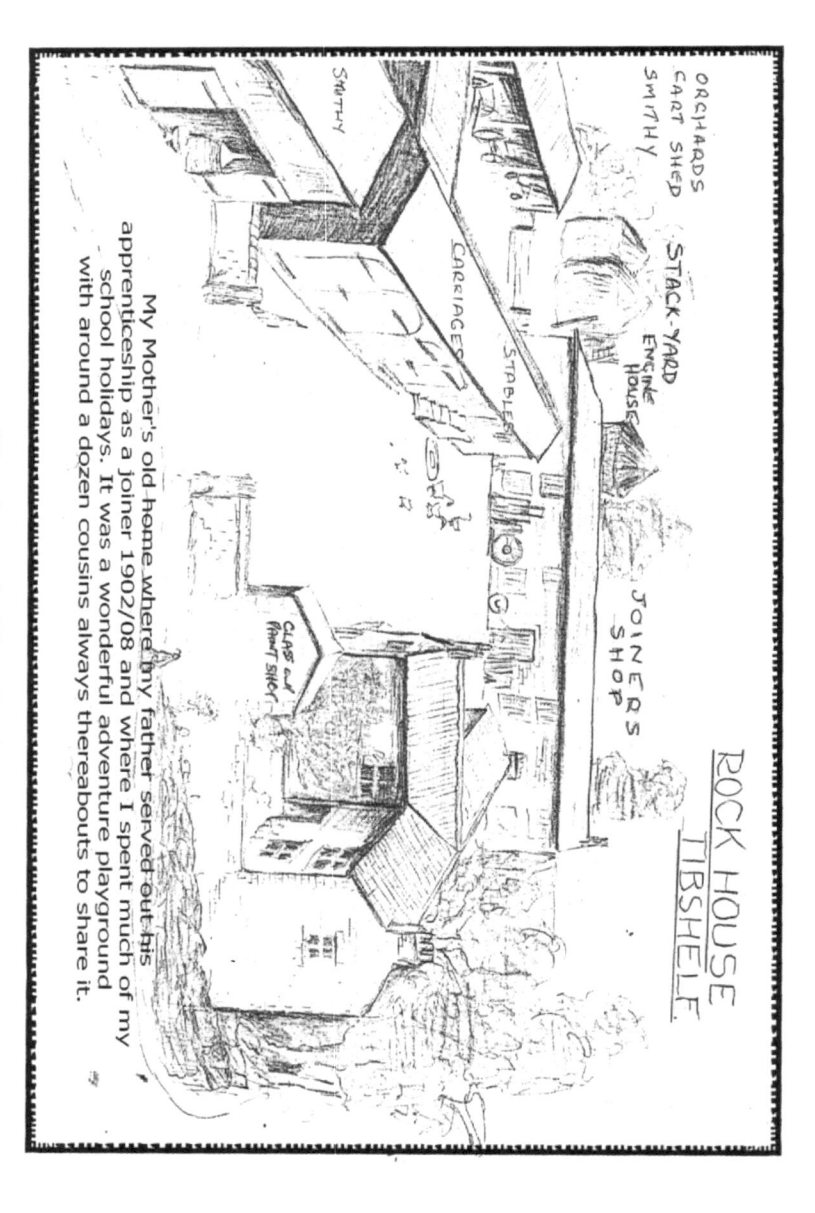

My Mother's old home where my father served out his apprenticeship as a joiner 1902/08 and where I spent much of my school holidays. It was a wonderful adventure playground with around a dozen cousins always thereabouts to share it.

The Author's Sketch of
ROCK HOUSE, TIBSHELF.

Chapter 2
The Smiths and the Turners

Mother was a Smith, Ellen Smith, daughter of George, granddaughter of John, that John Smith who in 1857 had left his native Quarndon, a few miles north of Derby and moved some twenty miles north to Cross Farm, Tibshelf and there Mother was born 17th September 1887. John's elder brother had been more adventurous; that same year 1857 he had sailed away to Australia with his wife and three young children, but of them more anon.

Quarndon had been the family home for generations. In the 1740s and 50s Thomas Smith and his wife Mary were bringing up a large family on the little farm at Park Nook, Quarndon, whose land bordered the great park of Kedleston Hall, seat of the Earl of Scarsdale. Part farmer, part smith and wheelwright, part supplier of heavy staging horses for the carriage of manufactures from the Midlands to London, his older sons Tom and William followed him in these trades. Benjamin, the youngest, baptised at Derby 18th January 1753, did what others of his family had done before him and went into service with his Lordship at the Great House. There he was married, at Kedleston Church, 23rd October 1776 to Anne Sowter of an old and respected Duffield family. Almost certainly Anne was already part of the Household. They did well by his Lordship, Benjamin eventually becoming butler at Kedleston, where he died 21st May 1815, at the very time that Napoleon, the scourge of Europe, having made his escape from Elba, was

The Author's Maternal Family Tree.

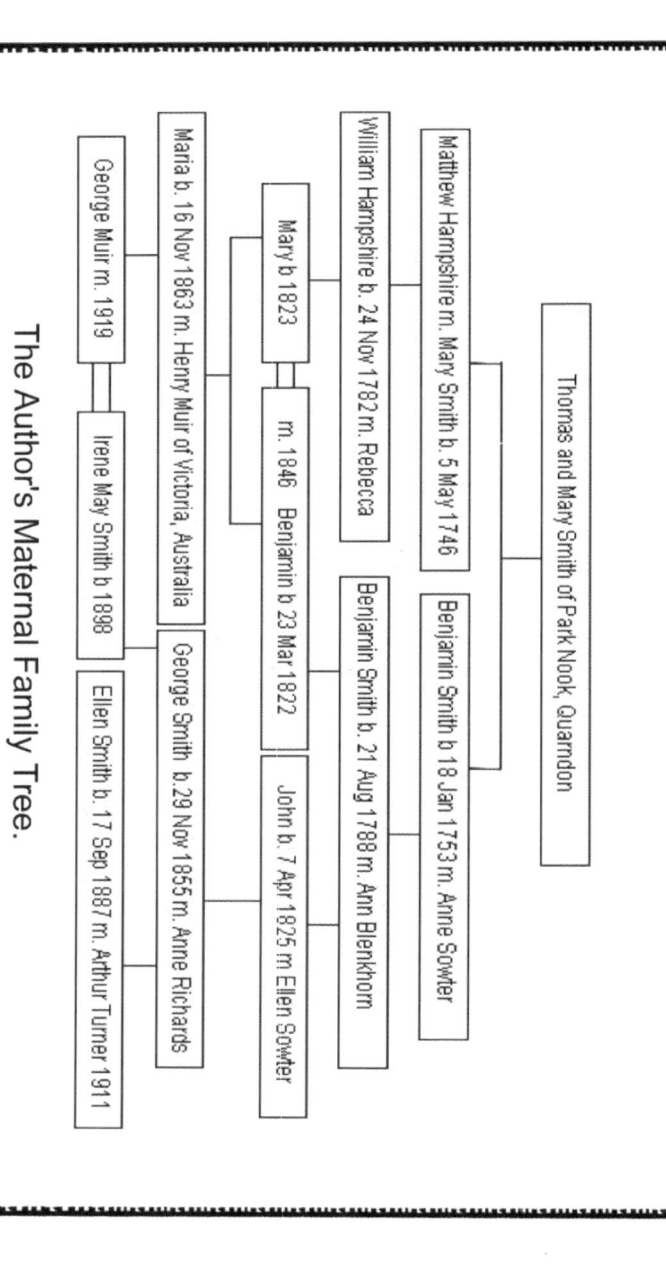

- Thomas and Mary Smith of Park Nook, Quarndon
  - Matthew Hampshire m. Mary Smith b. 5 May 1746
    - William Hampshire b. 24 Nov 1782 m. Rebecca
      - Mary b 1823 — m. 1846 — Benjamin b 23 Mar 1822
        - Maria b. 16 Nov 1863 m. Henry Muir of Victoria, Australia
          - George Muir m. 1919 — Irene May Smith b 1898
  - Benjamin Smith b 18 Jan 1753 m. Anne Sowter
    - Benjamin Smith b. 21 Aug 1788 m. Ann Blenkhorn
      - John b. 7 Apr 1825 m. Ellen Sowter
        - George Smith b. 29 Nov 1855 m. Anne Richards
          - Ellen Smith b. 17 Sep 1887 m. Arthur Turner 1911

43

rushing north from Paris, unaware that Fate had already made an appointment for him, three weeks later, with Wellington, on the battlefields of Waterloo.

Anne survived him by only a year, until 2nd October 1816, and they lie together with the Lords and Ladies, in the family graveyard at Kedleston. They also had reared a sizeable family of which the youngest, another Benjamin, born 21st August 1788, was brought up in his Lordships household and in due course became Agent and general factotum to the Kedleston estate. He was in all likelihood educated alongside the young Scarsdales in the schoolroom there, for his penmanship was immaculate and the formal correctness of his address beyond exception when he wrote proposing marriage to Mrs Ann Blenkhorn of Hagley Hall, Rugely, Staffs. Ann, as the courtesy title of Mrs. indicates was already a senior domestic at Hagley with Lord Curzon. That title had been granted around 1750 to Lord Scarsdale's brother, and Ben and Ann would often have met during visits exchanged between the noble cousins. Benjamin gently pleads that he has waited "until reaching the years of discretion and a position of sufficient consequence to permit himself to present his suit with dignity and yet with humility to a Lady so generously endowed with manifold virtues". My cousin, Mildred Greatorex of Newark (she was her great grandma as well as mine), has the letter, dated 19 October 1817; nowhere in it does Benjamin have the temerity to mention the word "love" or permit himself the liberty of addressing his intended by her Christian name. At all events the matter was brought to a fruitful conclusion, for between

1822 and 1836 they, in turn, reared a large family, and their second son was that same John Smith who left Quarndon forever in 1857 and became my Mother's grandfather, the Patriarch of the Smith's of Rock House.

Before we leave Kedleston we must mention the end of Benjamin, my great-great-Grandfather. Sadly Ben and Ann both died in his Lordship's service in 1836, probably in some epidemic of the day. Lord Scarsdale, seeing himself *in loco parentis,* assumed responsibility for the seven or eight orphaned children, all under 15 years old, getting the boys apprenticed and the girls placed in respectable service as they reached due age. Back in 1774, Ben's aunt, Mary had married Matthew Hampshire, also of Quarndon, and now, about 1838, John was apprenticed to his grandson William Hampshire, still at Quarndon, whose family were prospering in business as Bakers and Confectioners as well as wheelwrights and joiners. He was joined by his brother Ben, but at the end of their Articles they parted, John leaving for Tibshelf and his own establishment as Master-man, while Ben, who had been more interested in the Bakery, married his employer's daughter Mary Hampshire and set sail for Australia in 1857 with their little family aged seven, five and three. After an adventurous voyage they arrived safely and eventually settled at Christmas Hills, Victoria, on land they had taken up and called Park Nook after the old home far-away.

And here's another romantic little story of coincidence and the strange chain of events. Nearly sixty years after the landing,

Ben's grandson George Muir came to Salonika in the A.N.Z.A.C forces in 1915. There, somehow, he came upon some of Mother's brothers, fighting with the Australians against the Turks and came to England on leave with them to look up his distant cousins. He married their second youngest sister Mary and took her back to Australia and Mother has kept in touch with their four daughters, now all grandparents themselves, with lots of descendants, and as that is too tangled a skein to unravel I'll set it out more simply.

John Smith had married Ellen Sowter, kinswoman of his grandmother, and they came to Tibshelf with a one year-old son, George, my grandfather Smith. At the cross-roads on which Cross Farm was situated, one of the corners was a rocky outcrop raised some ten feet above the road, and on this the house was built. It was a substantial stone built T-shaped house, and, the fortunes of the Smith's being now in the ascendant, the house was renamed Rock House. Grandad told me once that this was his sister's doing; they were rather, what we would have called, stuck-up, educated in the somewhat rarefied atmosphere of dame schools, and urged that the new name was more suitable for a dwelling substance, occupied by so respectable a family! If so, how clever that so apt a name should be paced before a God-fearing Bible-reading clientele as the place of business of a Master-builder! Undertaking and blacksmithing were added to the joinery work, together with carriage hire, and in the later years of the Great Queen's reign, my grandfather took over a thriving and prosperous business. And to it came my father, second son of a busy farmer a few miles away who had no doubt been a customer; there were poor prospects for all three of his sons on the farm, so my father came to Tibshelf as apprentice, about 1901, indentured for seven years, at the end of which he upped and married his employers daughter, just as her great-uncle Ben had done at Quarndon in 1846.

My earliest memories of Rock House, the place Mamma called "home" were those of a tiny five year-old, hemmed in on all sides by grown-up legs and skirts, men in khaki, my uncles all back from foreign parts, all except Uncle Tom, and the girls, four of them counting Mamma, laughing and quarrelling and shouting their heads off and everyone arguing about everything under the sun. Hens under the table and the odd suckling piglet scuttling into its corner, it was all excitement, quite different from the ordered calm of Carr Farm.

By the time I was seven, every holiday I would set out to walk across the fields, three miles to Heath station and then three miles again by train to Tibshelf; a shilling for fares and a shilling to spend. Auntie Kathie was a booking clerk at Tibshelf station and she would ring down the line for them to look out for me at Heath and see me safe on to the train. As you came down the High Street, the Picture Palace on the right, Butcher Brown's on the left as you went past the Royal Oak and the Crown, then Richard's Yard on the left where Grandma Smith was born, then Morrell's farm, and there ahead after the mile-long trudge from the station, there was the gate of Rock House.

There were ten rooms not counting the attic bedrooms under the roof where Cousin Ben and I slept. Someone in their travels had brought home in a glass case a gigantic lizard - perhaps no more than three feet in reality but to my fascinated eyes then, nothing short of a full-sized dragon. Every night, creeping up to bed without a light, I would pluck up courage to steal past it at the top of the attic stairs, its eyes glinting in an odd shaft of moonlight through the loose tiles on the naked rafters, to take a flying leap onto the bed to bury myself under the sanctuary of the blankets. But in the morning what larks! A whole great chest of uniforms, busby hats with cockades and shining chin pieces, tunics scarlet and Connaught green with chain epaulettes and fancy gold and silver tassels to hang from the shoulders, sabres and saddlery, volunteer uniforms - relics of Grandad's days in South Africa and of the Yeomanry of Edwardian times. No wonder they were all Yeomanry mad, my mother's harum-scarum brothers, and small wonder too that even then the hook was baited and as soon as I was old enough I would be joining up myself.

As you came down to the gate of the yard, the house rose from its rock on the right surveying the business buildings about it. To the left of the gate stood the Blacksmiths-shop, then the carriage houses then the stables and the granary overhead. Just within the gate on the right was the glass and paint shop. Across the top of the yard filling the whole width of it was the joiner's shop. Away behind on the left, the cow-byre, the calf boxes, the implement yard, the engine house and the stack-yard and orchard beyond and then the paddocks. To the right the yard narrowed between the house and the joiners shop, leading through to the back entrance where you came out on to the Alfreton road. Behind the Shop was the kitchen garden and the greenhouse; every morning in August it would be my first task to pick a basin-full of the cream coloured raspberries that grew in profusion, but we hardly dared turn our eyes towards the greenhouse, heavy with Grandad's grapevine in full fruit, hanging ripe like apples in this Eden of my childhood.

It doesn't begin to describe it all. There were the smells of animals, newly cut timber and wood-shavings, stains, putty and paint, hay and apples, the grey-headed geese, the cackling of hens, the stamping of hooves and jingle of harness, the ring of the anvil and the smell of red-hot shoes being fitted to the horses feet, and there were the make-believe sounds of our daily round of adventure, the guns of the cowboys and the whooping of the Indians, the wind in the rigging of the windjammer harvest wagon, sword ringing on sword of the cavaliers and roundheads and maidens in distress that peopled our childish imagination.

If you go there now it's nearly all there still, the same house, the same walls and roofs under the same sky. But the magic of childhood is gone. There is no buried treasure under the roots of the oak tree in Samson's field, no secret passage underneath that pile of rocks in the back paddock as there was then. Cousin Benny was my constant companion; he lived with Grandma although he had a home and family of his own over Clay Cross way. He was two years older than me and if Grandma was out he would bring in his gang, the lads of the village, Alec Hall, Ernest Dearden, Harry Sellers, Cutty Sharp and that awful boy Sogger Pratt, alternatively rustlers and Indians, Chinese pirates, cruel Turks and naked Zulu's. And cousins Sid and Dorothy, Mary and Kathy, Theo. and Bert and Mabel. So many times I rescued Mary from cannibals and sinking ships; from forest fires and cattle stampedes and runaway stages that I fell in love with her when I was eight and it's lasted all our lives.

We would raid the orchard making a store of half-ripe apples to hide in the hay, roam down Sunny Bank and Doe Hill Lane, over to the Westwoods or across to Blackwell. There, at Uncle Bert's Church Farm we would picnic on Mount Sinai, just beyond the garden wall by the greengage tree, or sledge breakneck down it in the short sharp days at Christmas. There, at night, I'd sleep three-in-a bed with Mary and Kathy, lying sleepless into the small hours counting the quarter-hour chimes from the grey tower of the church across the paddock. Back at Tibshelf, when it rained we'd play hide and seek in the buildings, through the cattle shed loft, through the trap door into the carriage house where you could climb fearfully up onto the seat of the great twenty seater shillibeers beside the waggonettes and sheeted down funeral landaus. And above all the Shop - the joiner shop - the centre round which the life of Rock House revolved. Grandad's bench and Uncle Bert's bench, Uncle Arthur's, Uncle Ben's and Uncle Willie's, each with his separate place, his tools on the wall. Carts and wagons to make or repair, wood to be fetched from the station, sometimes great timbers to be hauled in on the huge, six-in-hand timber-drungs. There was glass to cut, horses to shoe, stools, chairs and tables to make and coffins. There were always coffins - beautifully smooth as you stroked your hands over the grain, fragrant with linseed oil; and the funerals to arrange, shining top-hats to be carefully taken out of their tissues, coats and driving sheets to be brushed, harness to be soaped and polished, horses to be groomed, even their hooves to be blacked and shone.

It was a village where, to my mind, it was natural that every now and again folk should suddenly topple ever and die. Grandma would come hurrying down from the Crown, gliding along like a ship in full sail, hot with news - Tom Reynolds has dropped down dead! That's how it was; they never seemed to keep anyone waiting! There being no telephones, not for ordinary folk, the pub was the centre of local news. Within minutes my grandparents would be decked in their second-best, Grandad with his rule in his inside pocket and Grandma to arrange the preparation of the body for its lying-in before the last and most luxurious journey it would ever make in this world. Together they would hurry up the street, while Uncle Bert would eye his stocks over his specks, rub his chin and speculate on whether it would be oak or elm for the coffin.

And wheels! Now there was a thing to see - to put the iron tyre on a cart-wheel. The wheel is assembled, nave, spokes and fellies morticed glued and cramped up. Then, on the day, it is laid flat on a great iron saucer six feet across. From the smithy comes the tyre, four or five inches wide, five-eighths thick, half or three quarters of an inch too small for the diameter of the wheel. Then, round its circumference you build a fire of all available off-cuts put by for the purpose, with coke and coal until the iron is red hot and you hold up your hands against the heat on your face. And lo and behold, the expansion of the iron under the heat has made it big enough now to slip over the wheel if you are snappy about it. So, at the given signal, with shouts of encouragement, four men with great iron pincers, north east south and west about, seize the red-hot tyre, lift it over the wheel and lower it to the rim, drop their pincers, grab the sledgehammers, and strike with all their might driving the tyre down into place before it has time to contract. The red-hot iron has set fire to the fellies of the wheel so, the instant it is in place, like soldiers in Wellington's squares, the second line steps forward with pails of water to douse the flames; and more water yet hurried from the pump by wide-eyed struggling eight year-olds, the reserve troops. The contraction of the iron under the cold water squeezes the joints together till the wood itself screams like a hare in a trap. Centuries ago must Isaac Newton have marvelled at it, at the terrible forces of nature harnessed by man out of the very universe. That wheel is so bound together that for a hundred years in rain or sun it will carry its daily load as sound as a bell. I tell you it was a thing to see; flames lighting up the yard, throwing leaping shadows of the men over the walls and their arms and faces scorched and drawn and soaked in sweat from the heat and the last ounce of their strength. And then the beer and the laughing voice of a girl fading away as drooping eyes shut out the world into dreams at last.

Just beyond the Royal Oak stood the Picture Palace, its name grandly carved out of Portland stone across its front. Yes, I was familiar with the Saturday afternoon penny rush at Bolsover, but now, under promise of never telling my mother, Grandma allowed me to go to the evening performance which as everyone knows is something quite different. People were picture-mad and every village of any size had its own, even there, miles from the nearest town there were four cinemas in a two mile radius. Too young in the early days to appreciate the great romantic actors of the day, I could now see the "Big Picture" with Valentino, Douglas Fairbanks, Mary Pickford, Ronald Coleman, Dorothy and Lillian Gish. Still it was the Western and Comedy two-reelers that really held us; Tom Mix, Pearl White, William Farnum, William Powell, Harold Lloyd, Buster Keaton, Fatty Arbuckle, Laurel and Hardy and of course Charlie Chaplin. The written captions that punctuated the silent films were chanted out loudly by all the youngsters and noticeably helped their reading. Dashing home in the dark, racing down the black street with a penn'orth of chips between the three or four of us, was a fitting end to those Saturday nights. Once a travelling company of players spent the week there and for the first time we thrilled to watch real life actors. "Maria Marten or the Murder in the Red Barn", "East Lynne", "In the Hands of the Mormons". But "Under the Surgeons Knife" was not for us - adults only, second house! With Elmo Lincoln we swung through the jungle of Tarzan's Africa and with Douglas Fairbanks strode with flashing blades through the adventurous days of the Three Musketeers.

I was already a keen reader. At home we had a few books, old passed-on Sunday-school prizes like "True to Her Faith" and one or two grown up best sellers of the day such as Hutchinson's "If Winter Comes". Mothers reading time was taken up with "Home Chat" or the serials in the Weekly Telegraph, all at tuppence each. Naturally Dadda had his "Farmer and Stockbreeder" and his one extravagance, Nash's. At Tibshelf Benny was luckier; he had the Rover, Adventure, Champion and Wizard either new or swapped, all of which would have been dismissed as rubbishing extravagance at home. Grandad had a whole bookcase of solid reading, a relic of the late Victorian years when a passion for learning swept the country; "Harmswoth's Self Education and Encyclopaedia" occupied one whole shelf with a dozen handsomely bound volumes, "British Battles By Land and Sea" in red relief leather-tooled in gold, bound volumes of "London Illustrated News on the South African War", the works of Shakespeare, Tennyson and Wordsworth. These were leavened by "Oliver Twist", "Uncle Tom's Cabin", "The Water Babies" and "Alice in Wonderland", and weighted down by my dreaded Sunday afternoon ration of "Pilgrims Progress". There I found my first grown-up novel "The Clannings" which I read from cover to cover with its sequel "Peter Yorke"; I enjoyed them both though I've never read them again, never seen them even, now I come to think of it. I lapped up Ballantyne's Gorilla Hunters and Coral Island and Kipling's "Stalky and Co..". Benny found a battered copy of the "The Blue Lagoon" which we read with baited breath in the secrecy of the hay-loft. And so, by the time I was twelve I was already quite a book-worm, and English Literature was by some way my most enjoyable and most complete school subject in later years, all started in that quiet drawing-room among the Harmsworth's "Self Educators". That really is where my proper childhood ended and where teen-age began, when the trailing clouds of glory melted away under the harsh light of my less happy school-days. Just before the summer holidays in 1924 I'd had news - my very first letter I shouldn't wonder - that I'd been successful in the County Minor Scholarship exam, entitling me to a free place at Chesterfield Grammar School. When I showed the letter to Gaffer Day at Welbeck Road that morning I was surprised to find myself a celebrity, standing alone and quaking before the assembled school, the only successful candidate of about forty. Quite half of the parents would not allow their children to attempt the exam as many working-class families looked no further than the elementary school for their children's education - 14 was considered the proper age to leave school and start work to contribute to the family purse. Those who did not get a free scholarship had a second chance to pass for a paid place, and this Arthur did pass though he had been left without a chance at the exam by a change in the age limits. For him this cost £10 for the year's tuition, about £2 per year for books and £3 per year for train fare, all of which I had for nothing. My cousin Ted Milner also passed the scholarship from Heath and we were together right through our days at Chesterfield. Kathy Smith, my Blackwell Church Farm cousin also passed for the

Girl's High School the following year so we thought a bit of ourselves with all the brains rattling around.

I cannot say I enjoyed the next six years as I had my earlier schooldays. I worked hard, as I had to, to hold my place in class in face of the stiffer competition I now find about me. I did quite well, progressing steadily and when Matriculation came round, when I was just 15, I passed in English, Maths, French, Latin, History, Geography and Physics, with my only failure Chemistry. We also did woodwork and art but in those days these were not considered serious subjects for the Matric! Our teachers were of a uniformly high standard, all being honours graduates of Cambridge or Oxford, and some of them were very good indeed. But they worked under a system that requires the level of exam success to govern the School's cash quote from the Ministry. Exam success was all. As a result the provincial grammar school's measure of success was to produce an unending stream of countryfied know-alls, overloaded with text-book learning, half educated in their own spoken language, quite ignorant of all civilised social graces, knowing nothing of music, the arts or the theatre, except for the dreadful annual school concert and Shakespeare play.

I enjoyed school games, rugger, cricket and boxing, getting into the 1st XV and the Cricket Eleven on a few occasions. I was boxing at 5 stone when I was already in the Sixth, so I had quite a bit of success against 11 year-olds. Although I was so small, my long journeys to school kept me fit. But latterly a shadow had crept over the horizon and in my last two years I became increasingly conscious of a periodic deafness that would come over me like a blanket for a day or two at a time. All those last two years I had the greatest difficulty in hiding this from my family, my teachers and my school friends. During my last summer at school in 1930 this deafness was more and more oppressive and I knew it was seriously affecting my work. In early July the Head had had me in to discuss my future, suggesting that with my farming background Forestry might be just the ticket, and if I spent another year at school I'd have every chance of an exhibition to Edinburgh University. And even in the unlikely event I did not get a grant my father was in a position to foot the bill!

All this I told my father that evening as he sat reading as usual before the kitchen fire. He wasn't really listening at first, and then it seemed to dawn upon him, and he told me to start again while he listened carefully and quietly. It wasn't in his nature to go off the deep end and roar the house down, but it came to me that he was having difficulty in keeping his temper. I was to get up the following morning in my working clothes, breeches and boots and make myself useful in the hay harvest, which was in full swing, and he would go to school in my place. It was the one and only time he ever went to my school. I never heard the outcome. I know he was furiously angry and at the time, in the depths of the worst farming depression of the century, was at his wits end to keep us out of queer street; milk was 6/2d a gallon and wheat was less than a ha'penny a pound.

I never went back to school. That was how it ended; school-days chopped off and working days begun overnight before I knew it. Before me were blistered hands, heavy clod-hopping boots, sun and rain and aching muscles, sweat and toil, and at the same time a happy release from the hardest working time of my whole life, my last school years, but never once have I been tempted to go back, or look back with nostalgia on the day I went through those iron gates for the last time. To a small boy, the Twenties were about motor cars and Jack Hobbs, Jack Dempsey and Dixie Dean, strikes and Steve Donoghue, skirts above the knees for the first time since the ancient Britons, American films and the coming of the 'Talkies'. Disciplines in the family and at school was strict but acceptable, it's not easy for our generation to see the benefits the lowering of these standards has brought. Arthur and I took it for granted that we should walk the sixteen mile return journey to Chesterfield School in the General Strike; we were excused attendance until 10 o'clock, which we thought a great privilege, but were granted no homework favours when we got home.

I think the generally lower standard of living threw people together making life a much more communal affair than it's possible to realise today. Children ran unaccompanied to school, women walked the night-black roads in safety, and lovers clung warm together in the country lanes, sharp under the moon and the winter frost. We looked forward to Christmas as now, even though our expectations were less. We possessed a thick Gamage's catalogue and spent hours dreaming over the pictures of pedal cars, doll's houses and prams, roller skates and clockwork trains, scooters, rocking-horses and the like, not enviously, just dreaming! There was more churchgoing, more carol singing, more pianos to thump out the hymns and sixpenny popular song-sheets. There was more visiting from house to house, farm to farm. Often enough my father and his neighbours have sat the night out playing ha'penny nap till breakfast.

Then on the other side of the coin, there was small-pox and diphtheria, tuberculosis and infant mortality. The Haslams' at Palterton - he was the foreman wagonner at Godber's farm - all died off, parents and all, Eva, Jack, Jim about seven of them until only Herbert the youngest was left. Everyone could tell of such sad cases of the savages of consumption. We saw more people drunk because drinking was in public and there was the money for it in the coal and steel. There were more flies, a hundred-fold, and we took the regular school examinations for fleas as a matter of course, and, as necessary, the tooth-combing ritual, head over the kitchen table, and once, at Grandma's, an embarrassed vinegar bath on the hearth.

Most people knew each other - "Eh up Jack! Now then Joe! Morning Ruth", good morning, good morning, even strangers passed the time of day. Children perhaps from shyness were more stony-faced. There was no work for married women except in shops or a bit of house cleaning - not many miners would allow their wives to go out earning money, it was beneath their dignity. For that reason the women ruled the home, assuming a natural degree of strength, competence and self-confidence that felt no need of the strident femininity of these modern protesting times, and the Flapper Vote arrived in the middle of the decade.

I forgot to mention the Mummers! Sixth January, Twelfth Night, the traditional night for the Mumming Plays. Back a couple of generations in Thomas Hardy's England they had traditionally been played by the younger ploughboys, the words passed down orally over many generations. Now they were, alas, reaching the end of their history, coming as some say from the Crusades or the Miracle Plays of the Middle Ages. Dad told me that many different versions had been brought out of Lincolnshire by the itinerant farm labourers of his youth. But by my time they had passed to the older schoolboys and at Tibshelf I always joined in with enthusiasm on the last Saturday night of the holidays. Not at home though. I was never allowed out of doors in the dark, but it did not prevent me helping at rehearsals in the comfort of the barn. From farm to farm we went, from pub to pub, taking in the more well off village folk, the butcher, the doctor, the schoolmaster, the parson and anyone who might be good for a sixpence or even a few coppers. The words come back over the years - perhaps I could give you an idea of how it went. And remember the costumes were paper and cardboard, make-up was soot, chalk and black-currant jam. Right then! Pray silence for Tom Fool and brave King George, the poor plow-boys and the wily Listing Sergeant, Old Mary and the Bold Prince, the indefatigable Doctor and Beelzebub the Devil's Sprite.

Tom Fool *(in a sort of Jester's costume)*
For I sing of the jolly plow-boys who labour all year long,
They come your favour to win
And with your consent they shall come in.

1st Plowboy *(country yokel style)*
In come I my whip in hand, as I go to plow the land:
Straightway go I from hedge to end, never make a baulk or bend.
Our back is broke our hands are sore
Help us poor weary plowboys for we can work no more.

2nd Plowboy
All year long we've toiled and moiled through all the muck and mire
So now we bring our seasons play as you sit round your fire.

Tom Fool
In this peaceful house tonight they'll tell you of the fearful fight
Between King George and the Black Prince bold
Before he leaves him dead and cold.
And if you don't believe these words I say
Come forward Sergeant and clear the way.

Sergeant
In come I the Listing Sergeant, list and do not be afraid
For I have orders from the King to list the plowboys aid.
We threshed Old Boney and his crew
And if you're not careful we'll thresh you too!

Tinker, Tailor, Pedlar, Nailer, with ten bright guineas for your pay
A gallant show and on we go if you will join your King today.

Plowboys *(taking the King's bounty)*
We two jolly plowboys but now we're called to arms
We'll die upon the battle-field or in a fair maids arms
For here's our Lord and Master now whose sword we bear today
Attention all! Step in King George, step forth and clear the way.

King George *(like St. George, silver crown and Red Cross on his shirt)*
I come I King George the Champion bold
I won ten thousand pound in gold
The fiery Dragon I brought to slaughter
And kissed the King of Egypt's daughter
I've travelled the world both round and round
But never my equal have I found.
And if you don't believe these words I say,
Step in Black Prince and clear the way.

(Enter B.P. like the King only all blacked up)

Black Prince
In come I Black Prince of heathen race
Black my heart as black my princely face.
This night I'll fight the King and Crown

And bring his life and courage down
(hiss, hiss!)
King George it is who standeth there
Slew Saladdin my master's heir
I'm going to have his royal blood
And make it flow like Noah's Flood.

K. George
Stand back thou black Moroccan dog
(aside) I do not fear the swinish hog.
 Put up thy sword or thou shalt die
 I swear I'll make thy buttons fly.

Bl. Prince
Thou canst not make my buttons fly
Who never has been heard to cry.
My head is made of brass my body made of steel
My knuckles are made of the best knuckle bone
And no man living can make me feel.

K. George
I'm the man to make thee feel

Bl. Prince
And I'm the man to show my steel.
I'll bash you and slash you as small as flies
And send you to Jamaica to make mince pies.

(They fight until the B.P. falls lifeless to the floor. In comes Mary and old, old woman)

Mary
King George, King George what have you done
You have killed and slain my only son
See how he lies all bloody on the ground -   *(Shouts)*
Five pounds for a doctor to heal his wound!

K. George
Ten pounds he stays away!

All
Fifteen pounds he must come!

Doctor
In come I who never cometh yet, the best quack doctor you have met
Straight from the Coutinong I came
To cure this man King George has slain.

Tom Fool
How came you to be a doctor?

Doctor
I travelled for it.

Tom Fool
Where did you go?

Doctor
Italy, Sicily, France and Spain
Over the hills and back again.

Tom Fool
And what can you cure?

Doctor
Hipsy Pipsy Palsy Gout, pains within and pains without
Are you a martyr to indigestion, rheumatics, sciatica, loss of direction?
Heart-burn and colds, belly that rolls
Pains in the back - floating spots before the eyes
My celebrated chest expanding brace will cure all ailments.

Tom Fool
But look, this man is dead!

Doctor
Heal the sick and cure the lame, bring the death to life again
Set a leg and draw a tooth and bring the dead to life forsooth
(Bends over the body)
He's in a trance, he is not dead
He's been living on potato tops and they've gone to his head.

Mary
If you can bring the dead to life
I'll pack my bag for a donkey's wife.

K. George
If he's a doctor I'm a sago pudding!

Doctor
I've got spectacles for blind bumble-bees
And crutches for lame duck's knees.
Hard corns, soft corns, pains in the big toe,
(looks at K.G)
And that's more than you can cure I'll have you know.

Mary
What is your fee kind sir?

Doctor
Usually five pounds but just for you I'll only charge ten
(Mary burrows into her skirts and some of the others chip in.
She gives him the money)
Now take three sips of this magic bottle
Down thy gory thrittle throttle
(with a flourish he pours it all over him)
And take these pills, two tonight and two tomorrow
And swallow the box at dinner time
(He empties the pills over him)

Black Prince *(Moaning, holding his head, Mary helps him to his knees)*
My back is broken
My head is sore

Never been known to happen before

Mary *(on her knees before the King)*
Your honour King George please set him free
I'm certain he's sorry as he can be -
He's my only son, I have no other
And always so kind to his widowed Mother.

K.G. *(takes the B.P.'s arm)*
Come, rise Black Prince, stand by my side
For I've a plan this Christmastide -
I swear I was never in a braver fight
And you shall be my chiefest Knight.

Beelzebub *enters in Devil's costume.*
In come I, Beelzebub, over my shoulder I carry a club.
In my hand a frying pan - don't you think I'm a jolly old man?

Buxom Lass
In come, I a lady fair, eyes so bright and golden hair.
My love has scorned my sweetest charms
And left my lorn with empty arms
He's off to fight on the desert sand
Listed for a soldier in a foreign land.

Beel.
Ten bright guineas I'll give to thee

If you'll pack your traps and come with me.
Dresses of gold and laces so fine
And bedding of satin and silk to recline.

B.Lass
Farewell Ploughboy, hello Sorrow
(To Beel.)
We'll call the Banns and wed tomorrow.

Chorus
Good Master and sweet Mistress, as you sit by the fire
Remember all poor ploughboys that plough through muck and mire;
Remember all poor lasses, fallen by the way
And spare a toast to all poor souls upon this Christmas Day.

Tom Fool
Gents and Ladies brave and fair
Here's an end to all despair
Thank you for your Grace this day
As you have listened to our Play.
Thank you for your Yuletide cheer
Thank you for this jug of beer.
And bear in mind our Pantomime
Peace and Goodwill this Christmastime!

 Now to tell you something about the Turners to give you an idea of how their lives were governed by the land, how its soil and animals dominated their whole existence. They came from many generations of tenants of the Dukes of Devonshire, and the great windows of the Duke's seat at Hardwick Hall reflected the setting sun across the valley to the hamlet of Astwith where Grandad was born and where his forebears had lived for centuries. Their name was on local maps of Tudor times and the Volunteer rolls of the time of the Armada.

Dad was one of six children, one of them Alfred dying young, Elizabeth, Olive, Cornelius, Arthur and Tom quite naturally all either married farmers or farmed themselves. Aunt Bessie, fat and merry, had two daughters; she was the widow of George Stubbins of North Lodge Farm on which Shirebrook Colliery was built. George was quite well off but he either shot or hanged himself, I'm not sure which, before I was old enough to know anything about it. Aunt Olive married George Milner and brought up two sons at Ivy Farm, Heath, just down the village street from where I was born. Uncle George had an enquiring mind, a bookish man but an idle one who read the daylight hours away by the fire while his wife milked the cows, kept the hens and hawked the eggs and butter from door to door at Doe Lea. Ted and Frank, my contemporaries, were both talented ball-players; they both became teachers and are comfortably off in retirement: Ted still lives at Heath where he has spent his seventy years and Frank, now alas broken down with arthritis, is still no more than three crow's miles from his birthplace. Uncle Corney, bearing the old family Christian name, married Elizabeth Wood, daughter of a Langwith farmer, and lived at Bassett Farm, Upper Langwith, where

Grace and I spent the war-time years after Uncle Corney had moved a mile down the road to Apsley Grange. Strangely enough, Grace had been under-nurse to the Apsley children on the Bathurst Estate at Cirencester Park. Uncle Tom married Nellie Saunders his second cousin and their two sons, Fred and Geoff, still farm in partnership at the Elms Farm, Palterton where Grandad had moved in 1890. Dad had stayed at school at Scarcliffe till he was fourteen, having to pay tuppence a week for his tuition for the last two years. Leaving school, he became a butcher-boy for two years at Bolsover becoming a competent dresser of carcasses and curer of bacon which came in useful in later life when he killed a pig or when a sheep broke a leg. Tiring of that, as I have already told, he became at 16 apprenticed joiner and wheelwright at Rock House. When he and Mother were married it was a bit of a toss-up what trade he should settle in; almost inevitable you will say, they decided on farming at Yew Tree Farm, Heath.

I am really trying to show that even a few years back you would find people in tight family groups living on the land, the same land, hardly moving a half-days walk over the years, over hundreds of years even. Do you wonder that it becomes part of their very nature? They have laboured for it, gone hungry for it, caressed it, fought for it. From it they have drawn their life-blood and back to it they will return, drawn irresistibly back from the ends of the earth.

Grandad was just retiring from a successful life's work on the farm and in the community about him, and was now passing on one of the best farms for miles around to his youngest son. He was a founder member of the Farmer's Union and of the Shire Horse Society. He was the local Collector of Taxes and an opinionated committee man with a wide circle of acquaintance, chairman sometime of Chesterfield Rural District Council and Justice of the Peace. He was a shortish, sober, pipe-smoking, non church-goer, very conscious of his local standing, a very fit seventy year-old of a somewhat pugnacious nature and not much sign of a sense of humour. Grandma was two years older, the daughter of Farmer Saunders of the nearby village of Teversal: almost contemporary with Mrs Beeton, she was a superb housewife of her time, a non-stop worker; wonderful cook, her house like a new pin. In her early years of marriage she has been used to making her own soap and candles and was still expert at home-brewed stout. She must have been very pretty then, and now, after more than fifty years since her wedding day, she was still a loving, lovely person. A gentle kindness shone in her eyes and she always had some sweetmeat or other for the grandchildren paying their duty visits of a Sunday. We were very fond of her though we trod very lightly with Grandad. She died quietly in 1944 at 89, the 66th year of her marriage; he lived on another six years and led his family a bit of a dance in his cantankerous declining years.

One of his friends was the general manager of the Shirebrook Colliery Company, and through him it was arranged that I should start work, down the pit, as a student underground surveyor. As with his own sons he saw that three sons on one farm could be one too many, and in a time of desperately high unemployment, this opportunity was a Godsend.

Chapter 3
Working for a Living

On the appointed day I set off at 5.30 a.m. on the five mile bike ride to the pit-head to catch the 6 a.m. 'cage' journey, five hundred yards down to the pit bottom, and thence through the miles of tunnels and galleries that made up the Colliery workings. The surveyors kept the records of these workings to keep the headings pointed in the right direction, check the measurement of the faces worked, the settlement of the roof, water leakage, gas and so on; when you cut through into another working, you were responsible for finding yourself in the right place.

Pits are not cosy places. Near the bottom the walls were bricked and whitewashed, brightly lit with permanent wiring, warm and dry. But out in the workings, maybe a couple of miles out the walls are rough black rock, laden with coal dust, the roof sometimes leaking water like a thunder storm, the air hot and foul, the toilet facilities non existent, the nearest space to be found. At the face there was the unnerving noise and commotion of the winning of the coal, but out in the old workings where we spent a lot of our time, we were out of earshot of anyone, with only the sound of dripping water, falling stone, the scurry of a rat, the groan of the roof, distant dull explosions of the shot-firers echoing mysteriously along the 'roads'. When you were quite alone except for a twinkle of light from a companion's Davey-lamp a hundred yards away, the pit is a weird place indeed.

At Palterton, wherever you turned, there were pit-head stocks with their winding gear and the black slag heaps against the sky, and thousands and thousands of men were working beneath out feet, sometimes in five or six seams, one below the other, the Tophard, Waterloo, Blackshale, Deep Soft, Low Main and so on, deeper and deeper beneath the surface, but each progressively shallower in themselves. Some were no more than three feet high so that men had to lie in their shoulders to pick out the coal, shovel it on to the conveyor-belts or into the steel tubs, to be clipped on to the endless steel haulage ropes that pulled them to the pit bottom, to be run into the cage, to be flung upwards into the light of day again at last after all of those aeons of time down there in the dark.

But for me it did not last long. My enthusiasm was soon brought to nothing. The change in pressure during the drop of the cage to the pit bottom is much more severe than any lift, and try as I might I found it impossible to relieve the pressure on my ears by yawning or swallowing or blowing my nose, and back came the deafness, much more severe than ever before. For whole shifts at a time I could hear very little, especially from a distance, and I suffered headaches of a severity such as I had never known or have ever experienced since. Eventually I had to report sick and my career as a mine surveyor came to abrupt end within a few weeks. Back I went to the farm again.

I've never regretted those five weeks. I saw coal-winning as a bitterly hard life to which generations of men have been born without thought of a change; it breeds bitter, hard men you would not cross lightly. But contrawise it also nurtures that clannish comradeship that men find in war or on the seas. Living so, they know themselves to be men apart, not as other men, finding fellowship and humour in the harshest experience, and, when the need arises, that high courage that comes naturally to men at war, or on the sea, or down the pit.

I do not suppose that I was very different from many a lad brought up in the all-pervading atmosphere of his father's livelihood. I had vowed to myself that whatever job I should undertake it would have nothing in common with working on the farm; that had always been a holiday duty and had become a lifetime's prospect to avoid like the plague.

I can only guess that my short sojourn underground and the relief at finding myself once more out in the open air must jointly have persuaded me that the land was by no means the meanest place to provide me with a living. It was some kind of haven in those hard days. The papers were full of accounts of millionaire bankers jumping off the roofs of the skyscrapers of New York and the popular song of the moment was "Brother can you spare me a dime". Farming suddenly looked a brighter goal.

I was born knowing something about it, or so it seemed; that you sowed the seed after ploughing and cultivating the ground, some of it wheat, some barley, some oats; that you had some crops to feed the animals in the winter and grass to feed them in the summer: that summer brought the hay harvest and autumn, the corn. I've never quite got used to the idea that there are grown people in the cities who don't even know what I'm talking about! What I now grew into was hard physical competition with my brother, with neighbours; competition in work to match the games competitiveness I'd always had. When I came in for lunch, after my first morning's muck-carting, my hands were covered with blisters as big as shillings, but Dad sent me out again for the afternoon to carry on with a quarter of a pound of lard to help me through to tea-time.

I now set to work to match my brother who, all his life, was a work fanatic. There was this film out about then, this new talking picture called "The Singing Fool" - well, Arthur was a working fool! But the harder the competition, the greater the advantage to the competitor. Where he could carry a twenty stone sack, I would at least carry eighteen; if he threw up three hundred sheaves in ten minutes then I would stack them: I would at the least fill four cart-loads of muck an hour to his five. I was learning the hard and best ways, from the best, for all his life, until the weeks before he died, in his seventieth year, he reckoned himself the best and never tired of proving it. If we hadn't each other then we'd match ourselves against the clock and every new record made was a record to break. Lots of our friends took us for twins but the fifty weeks that separated us sometimes seemed very long ones. Still it was the time of youth beginning to break into the strength of manhood and was just what I needed. As work came easier, so did play. I held my own at tennis, played in the boy's club teams at cricket and football. I'd scarcely bowled a ball at school but here I was getting a hat-trick for a local village team.

I began to study the diet of animals, experimenting with various feeds to get the cheapest but most palliative protein content in the meal mixes. Not the cheapest, the comparative cheapest! I soon found out that if you want the best from your stock you've got to give 'em the best. I persuaded Dad to buy a second-hand wool weighing machine from the local Viyella factory and adapted it to weigh the fattening pigs every week, to work out the weight gain against feed cost. Keeping the records, I was stumbling untutored into real costing, setting a firm foundation to a proper accountant's view of the farming business.

By the beginning of 1931 I was much changed from the schoolboy of six months before. Even academically I surprised myself, picking up my old set books again and wondering how on earth I'd have the nerve to take exams in books I had no recollection of ever having read. One day, ploughing, I learned Lamartine's "Le Lac de Bourget" by heart and after fifty years I haven't forgotten it, I read Thackeray and Hardy and discovered Surtees. Barrie's plays and Ibsen and Shaw. I believe these are peaks and valleys of physical as well as mental development, especially in the teens; you need help to bridge the valleys but you should take the crests flying, flat out, as long as your strength holds out. The hard physical work was filling me out too. I was getting out more in the evenings, joining a youth club at Bolsover, meeting last year's school friends, getting in the club football team and doing quite well at boxing - I was still a fly-weight! I had not much interest in girls save for a bit of shy sparking about on Sunday evenings coming home from Church.

It was shortage of cash that brought about the next change in my life. I needed a new bicycle but I had no money. At home I was working only for my keep - I never at any time drew a day's wages from my father. I had the keep of my one fat pig, worth £5, which I could cash in three times a year. But, brought up on the principle that however low your income you lived within it, I lived on five shillings a week for clothes and sundries and saved a shilling. I did not smoke and never went inside a pub, so it could be done; every year a new suit, two new shirts, one new pair of shoes, and working clothes, grey flannels, tennis shoes, football boots, all for less that £10. Anyhow, one way and another I was very alive to any chance of improving my income and when I heard of a vacancy for a student uncertified teacher I was keenly interested. This was a species now long extinct but in those days comprised the great bulk of elementary school teachers whose pupils left school at fourteen. They did not go to college or pass any teaching exam with pen and paper, the whole of their training being in the classroom, gradually progressing from a kind of superior monitor, accumulating teaching experience until they were good enough to 'go solo'.

I applied for a job and got it, at the same school where as an eight year-old I had done my sums and writing with a squeaking slate pencil ten years earlier, under the same Mr Haddock who'd given me four of the best that painful day in 1921. As I think I have already said, he was an outstanding producer of scholarship boys and was equally brilliant at producing teachers. I doubt if any comparable period in college now-a-days would prepare a young teacher to the same degree as twelve months under Mr Haddock. So I learned my trade as an artisan does, with the advantage of having an excellent boss, until he judged me fit to turn out into the wider school world on my own. And so I found myself in my first and only job as uncertified teacher of over fifty ten and eleven year-olds, boys and girls at the village school at Holymoorside, a picture postcard village a few miles to the west of Chesterfield where the Baslow Road climbs up on to Beeley Moor before dropping down to Chatsworth. I also got my first motor-bike, a 250 c.c. New Imperial, on the strength of my now fabulous income of thirty five shillings a week!

But, alas, the disability that I'd tried to forget for two years was there still and like a stifling blanket the hovering deafness came down on me again. Within three months I was attending hospital daily for treatment, all that early summer getting steadily worse. Teaching was done with by the time I took to a hospital bed with the outside world a dull mumble in my ears. And then, after my first visit to an operating theatre I woke back in the ward to a totally silent world! At first I had only a pad (one of those magic pads of waxed and carbon paper that you clean off with a shutter-slide) for communication. But within weeks came the first whispers of sound back again, and they sent me home fit enough to help in the corn harvest which in early September was in full swing. The hard outdoor work once more turned out to be excellent therapy and I soon began to improve. It was not until Christmas that I could persuade myself that the deafness had gone. Thank God it has never returned.

In the meantime those eight months had been a traumatic experience in the family and among my friends. I found it very embarrassing to meet people I had not seen for several months who had not heard of my handicapped state, and I suppose it helped me to bury myself in the work on the farm as the seasons came round. Harvest over, there was the autumn ploughing to be done. Muck-carting followed to clear the yards for housing the winter feeding cattle within the sheltering walls. That manure would go on to the frozen fallows for next spring's root crops that would be feeding the yarded cattle in twelve month's time, and so the never ending rotating farming year went on. I had never left it to go teaching. It had always been understood at home that I should continue getting up at 5.30 a.m. to feed and groom the horses and feed the sixty pigs and the same again in the evening. In addition it went without saying that the seasonal peaks of farm work took precedence over any leisure claims of my own.

By now we had a brand new Fordson tractor, but I was not allowed to lay hands on it as it was considered to be Arthur's exclusive property. From then on he washed his hands of any interest in animals and became a machine man. So it was just lucky for me that I now became horse-man (traditionally the senior job on all arable farms) only because there was no-one else to do the job. Dad ran the farm, giving any necessary orders, doing all the buying and selling; Arthur milked the cows (until George got old enough) and drove the tractor: I worked the horses doing any cultivation the tractor could not cope with, tended the pigs and helped with the yarded cattle. George was set to leave school the following Easter and join in the work generally.

Dad's job was the sheep which had the advantage of taking him and the dogs, Nell and Glen, about the farm every day. Even in summer when they feed themselves they still need seeing and counting everyday, the ewes, the flock matrons who provide the annual crop of lambs, the growing female lambs or gimmers, the older male lambs or wethers, and the shearlings that have survived the butcher into their second year. Dad ministered to their needs, delivering the lambs, trimming the feet against foot-rot, cleaning the maggots out of their open sores when they were 'struck by the fly', dosing or drenching them against worms and other parasites. He knew each ewe individually, the leaders, the bullies, the fence-breakers, the stragglers, each with a character of its own, and for any necessary help, say at dipping time, he had the daily companionship of his inseparable sheep-dogs. Now, harking back to his single days at Tibshelf he took on all the joinery and building repairs. Household gardening, lawn mowing, calf-rearing, poultry tending, hedging and painting all took up their quota of labour. There would be each year for sale £100 worth of lambs, £250 fat beast, £300 milk, £200 surplus corn, £400 fat pigs, and £30 surplus hay. Outgoings were to buy feed, new implements, repair materials to plant and buildings. No wages! Arthur had a share of the fat beast; I had the progeny of one sow, with luck £80 a year.

1932 was probably the deep point of the Great Depression. A hard year for everyone, but perhaps more so for our villagers then most townsfolk, since the only places of work for us were the pits and the farms. Those miners lucky enough to be in work at all were doing two shifts work and four days dole, or 'three and three' at best. In the busy times of harvest we often worked sixteen hours a day and the miners were grateful for the odd days of casual farm work at tenpence an hour. They had massive shoulders and enjoyed showing off their strength even if they had to break a pitchfork to do it.

That dark year turned and February 1933 brought the biggest snow blizzard I ever remember. It was a bitterly cold day with a cutting black gale coming out of Lincolnshire that Friday, and as the snow started, about two in the afternoon, I was hurrying out to the Hunger Hills with old Violet and the last load of muck for the day. We came to the large heap in the field and in minutes I flung off the load, threw down my fork, grabbed the reins and pulled left round the heap for home. Only too willing, Violet turned round short, ran the inside wheel halfway up the heap and over we went! I picked myself up and jumped to sit on Violets head where she was struggling

CORNELIUS TURNER
aged 21/22

on her side still yoked into the shafts, and suddenly all was quiet except for the moaning of the wind and the swish of the drifting snow. I had to get her out of the shafts somehow without leaving a broken legged mare on my hands! I had no knife to cut the harness, the buckles were all on the other side of the mare. A sharp stone? Already we two were just a white heap against the driven snow, and then, as I was working it out that no-one would be coming up here until Monday morning, through the blanketing snow came the rattle of a horse and cart. It was Arthur! he'd decided as usual not to pack up without doing one more load than I (can you imagine how infuriating it was to work with such a man) and here he was thumpety-thump across the field. Together we soon had the mare out, the cart on its wheels and turned for home. That snow kept on non-stop for three days!

Mother, who could be just about as mad as Arthur, decided to go to Derby the following day, Saturday, to the W.I. annual meeting or some such. Coming home in the dusk by train and bus she found the road blocked at Hillstown and set out to walk the last mile home. She would never have done it had she not come up with a miner fighting his way through the drifts trying to get to work at Glapwell pit. They struggled through the night and the drifts together, fortunately knowing enough to get clear of the road and take the open fields where the snow was partly scoured away. They finally reached our back door about ten at the point of exhaustion. It was a night my mother would never forget. We gave the miner a good supper and a sofa for the night and of he went after breakfast back home to Hillstown. I don't think we ever even knew his name. The village was completely cut off for the next ten days to road traffic. So far as we were concerned the stock was, as ever, the first consideration. Many sheep were buried for a week or more and one or two died. But they don't die easily, and we found them, one by one with often only a tiny pink breath-hole in the snow surface to locate them. The dogs were wonderful, working themselves to a standstill as some of the pit-men's' terriers did too, some were off their legs for days afterwards. As for the sheep, some of them had a healthy crop of lambs only a few weeks later. Never say die!

That Spring I had my first ploughing match. Dad had done no ploughing for years but he was a good tutor and Arthur had already won the lads' class. Now he was among the men in the tractor class and it was my turn with the horses. I did extra practice and of course I had a top-notch team in Blossom and Violet - they already had ten years experience before I started! Man and beast worked together to produce a furrow that should be straight as a taut line over the two hundred yard length of the work, all surface rubbish tidily buried, the plough set to produce a level finish that required the minimum of further cultivation to produce a seed-bed for the corn. In the autumn and on the clay the plough would be set differently, turning up a rough surface that would catch the frost which breaks the soil into the perfect tilth with the coming of the first daffodils. We both came in second that year and I never did get the first prize, though for years my brother travelled miles pot-hunting.

When you consider that every arable acre must be ploughed at least once a year and that a hundred acres of horse-ploughing takes twenty weeks, you will see that ploughing took up a considerable part of the work on the land in those days. But I never found it boring, the endless plodding back and forth. Rather I took a never failing pleasure in swinging the heavy plough round, sweetly balanced, at the headlands, talking to the horses, "gee-back, erve-a-bit", until there was no need to put any weight on the reins. No furrow was so straight it could not be improved on, especially with the sort of forthright critics that used to lean over my fences. I still hear the peewits in the autumn dotting the fallows in hundreds, and the screaming seagulls playing leapfrog about my feet over the slither of living earth endlessly turning under the plough breast. The harsh call of the rooks over the freezing furrows in the short days of midwinter, and the "gone away" of the huntsman's horn as I dashed to the heads of the excited horses as the hunt swept by; lords and ladies out of another world. It seemed to me the perfect job, in which you lost yourself in the life of the earth itself. Twenty miles a day, day after day, week on week were no conscious effort, no hardship, the body strong and tireless and much at peace.

There was the spreading of fertilizer from a hopper on the chest with a shoulder harness, like the biblical sower, striding over the land, arms swinging in rhythm, alternatively casting the gritty manure from side to side. Of course we had machine drills, but the horses were sometimes wanted elsewhere, and it was cheaper and did less damage to the growing corn, but it was really heavy work that had you watching the angle of the sinking sun towards the end of the day. The heavy work had become a challenge to meet head-on, you mastered the task. You will perhaps think all this much ado about nothing, an unsophisticated, uncouth, countrified attitude to life; but there it was! you can but learn by example. Those were the sort of standards we had to measure ourselves against, and if they got you through hard times without whimpering you were no worse a man for all that!

That spring, Captain came into the stable to start his life's work much as I was doing, his is a story on its own. The horses were my favourites, and of all the horses I ever knew, Captain stands unforgettably apart.

Chapter 4
Juvenile Delinquent

When my father had married and started out to farm on his first fifty acres at Yew Tree Farm where Arthur and I were born, the first two shire foals he'd reared at the same time had been Blossom and Violet. Blossom was the plain, barren maid-of-all-work, a much loved and devoted servant. Violet was the beauty, the spoiled matron, producing a fine foal at least every other year, winning lots of prizes at the local shows over the years. By the time she was seventeen, matriarch of the stable, she was put to Uncle Tom's stallion that had been Champion of All England, they must have known that neither of them could breed much longer. As it turned out he was her last foal, the last and best. That summer they'd trotted and strutted before the judges at the County Show and come out at the head of the line for the red rosette and the Champions Cup. But now, two later years on, here he was, newly housed in the stable, magnificent in his pride and strength, as only a shire can be, a bright bay giant of eighteen hands. You'd have thought he was born with a silver bit in his mouth.

Not quite a gentle giant. Violet could show a bit of a temper and show her teeth, so on Dad's advice I gave Captain the stall opposite the stable door, and I soon enough found the strength of that when he kicked me clean out on to the manure heap outside. It made a softer landing than being brought up hard against the stable wall, but I still have the scar on my jaw to remember it by. But there was no malice in him and in no time

Captain the Foal
"The Juvenile Delinquent."

at all he grew used to being groomed and handled and harnessed, having his tail and mane plaited, used to my voice, my hands, my boots on the stone sets. I had to stand in the manger to get his collar on the day we put him into the shafts for the first time.

Out on the Grey Banks there was a ten-acre piece of hay-rakings to get in and Dad had decided to try him out in the horse-rake and do a few turns round the field before loading up the wagons. As a precaution we packed the rake with hay beforehand to hold him back. There was the flick of a nerve on his quarters as the shafts were gently lowered onto his back but in a minute or two he was ready. I took the seat, reins taut, Dad on his bridle on the right and Harry Flint over the left and very gently off we went. But within a few yards his head was up and back, his eyes showing white; then his great feet were paddling short and fast, the sweat breaking out as an uncontrollable shivering seemed to possess him. His gathering speed was too much for Dad. He let go the bridle and threw himself headlong to his right to clear the steel teeth of the rake behind him. We hit a pothole and I was bumped clear out of the seat, somersaulting backwards, picking myself up in time to see old Harry fall asprawl in the path of the rake. The wheel hit him, throwing it high in the air; the teeth missing him by inches as it came bumping down again. Captain with a strangled neigh, bucking and kicking was off on his own tearing away like a wild thing at full gallop over the ley.

He must have been terrified; those wheels chasing him, this

clanging, clattering weight holding him back. Poor Captain! lumps of steel and splintered wood flew in all directions about him as he measured the length of the field and back to pull up panting before my outstretched arms, a lather of sweat, eyes staring, his whole frame ashake, half his harness gone and nothing at all left of the rake but half a shaft dragging behind him in the wreck of the traces.

Harry had taken the worst of it and we got him home on the wagon. It was Christmas before his bones were mended, but he was never the same man again, never went back to work with the ponies down Bolsover pit. Dad and I were right as rain. And Captain! Well I told him off good and proper when we got back. I really went at him with the curry-comb and dandy-brush, but he nodded his head, rattling his halter chain and pushing his nose at me like a penitent dog. I suppose I was barmy with him, but I'd never struck a horse in my life and this seemed no time to start.

Within a week or two we were in the corn harvest and it was decided to try a different plan. The lay-out of the stack-yard left a lane just wide enough for a wagon with stacks on either side, with the main house drive across the end with a high stone wall opposite. We loaded a wagon with corn; two tons of it there could have been, pointed towards the stone wall with no turning room. The rear wheels were secured with brake chains, and they stood back wiping sweaty hands on trouser seats as I brought Captain out. I'm sure he knew something was afoot but I talked away quietly to him and there were plenty of willing hands to help getting him into the shafts. But already there was a lather on him and the fear of the Devil in his eyes. The load behind him was a dead weight on chained wheels, no turning right or left, with a six foot stone wall in front of him ten yards away. Just teach him you can't always run away; let him tug and strain and break his heart; bring him to his knees; let him get it out of his system.

With a crack the hame-chains snapped tight and as he took the strain he was like a creature possessed. His quarters were down, the great muscles bunched grotesquely beneath the soaking skin; a stifled whinney came out of him and he was moving. Sparks and stone flew from the steel-shod hooves and he scrabbled for a foothold as he gathered way. I jumped back from his head as he came up to breast the wall, his momentum carrying him through it until he came to a standstill with its ruins around him in a choking cloud of dust.

There won't be many now-a-days who recall that day nearly fifty years ago. How for a moment no-one moved into the mess of steaming sweat and stone dust. "Steady lad, steady boy!" - I jumped for his head - "Whoa then boy! Steady, steady now!"; my voice sank to a whisper as I held his trembling head against mine, trying to soothe the tormented nerves till the sharp edge of them quietened and the terror left his eyes.

We got him out of the mess and as we strode back to the crew-yard they walked in file on either side with hurried steps and a skip now and again to keep up with us, telling it over to each other, fixing it in their minds to tell it over tomorrow, next week, next year. As for me, my arms goose-fleshed, my scalp on edge, was there a secret pride that it was my hand that held the bridle, that it was I pretending not to notice the huge hooves stamping down within an inch of mine? It was I who moved so intimately and carelessly about the massive quarters stripping off the harness and drying him down, but I had nothing to say for my throat was full.

As the word had gone round earlier that day, Uncle Tom had turned up, just happening to be passing, and propping himself against the gossiping wall, fore-armed against sympathy or compliments, with sarcasm and derision at the ready. Just the Northern way of showing family affection, but his cackling laugh was never far away and he was always prepared to take as good as he gave. As a grown-up to whom we could answer back he was a great favourite with us youngsters.

"Bad job then eh!" His boots scraped over the smooth worn sets of the stable floor, as he swaggered up, looking the horse over, his thumbs hooked in the arm-holes of his waistcoat. He swung to the left and right to draw the spectators with him. "Trying to ruin a good horse then! Not a bad sort of horse that, if he wasn't ruined." He paused to let it sink in, looking the horse over again, stepping up to him and giving him a sharp slap on the rump and swaggering back again.

"Pity eh! Pity you didna give the job to somebody as knows a bit about it!"

"Worth nowt now! Not worth a tinkers cuss!" It had the ring of a cheap bid in the offering, and some were sharp enough to let him know they'd rumbled him.

"Nay, nay! I don't want him now" he protested. "No use for him. But you don't like to see a good horse ruined. I'd have made a better job than that if he'd been mine. Tell you what I'd have done - tell you what I'd have done for a couple of quid - I could have had him gentle as a lamb in a week if I'd the time. Wouldn't know him in a week! Couple of quid eh! Gentle as a lamb."

It was a well-judged exit, leaving you with just enough to think over; and that was how Captain came to the binder episode. There was no gainsaying the fact that he was the most knowledgeable farmer in the village with horses. He'd taken over where Grandad left off with the best animals for miles. And Sid Wilson, his wagonner, was the best in the village.

He had a good sized piece of late corn to cut by the water-tower. They'd been round it half a dozen times before being held up by the weather, so it was nicely opened out and Sid had these two old mares in his stable so staid and set in their ways that nothing short of Doomcrack would put them off their stride. So one afternoon they yoked them, three abreast, in the binder, Captain in the middle. I'd heard nothing about it until I'd come home to lunch and heard Sid had been round to collect Captain, so I was late on the scene and only saw it from just inside the gate as I dropped my bike against the fence, they were a fair way off, down beside the straight edge of the standing corn, far enough to make the distance and the carrying of sound lend it an unreal feel of slow motion. There were men at the horses' heads. A single shout as they let go and stepped back. They were facing me, coming up the side of the corn. More shouts, the binder swung clumsily to the left into the corn, then right again among the stooks. Something was wrong with the traces and the huge machine seemed to take on a tilted look like a hen with a broken wing. It veered round in a half-circle and stopped. There was a crack of splintering wood and the horses were away. Sid was catapulted from his seat as for a second or two he clung to the reins and then they were free. Off they went, heels flying, through the corn and the open ground beyond, through the hedge as if it wasn't there, heads still reined together, the binder-pole dragging and leaping between them, feel-trees clattering behind them at the end of the traces. They were the best part of a mile from home, but they went for it in a bee-line, neither crops nor roads, fences nor wire were checking them. I was on my bike by now, and was the first to come up with them as they fetched up in my uncle's stable-yard, still roped together. The foaming lather of sweat was streaked with blood, streaming from the wire gashes about their legs, their bodies heaving with exhaustion and all of a tremble with shock.

Somehow I got him home, away from the storm of language and temper that fell on both our heads, and as I plodded home I felt overcome with helplessness and a dread of what the future might bring. I didn't really count for much, just the lad that did him. Horse-breaking was mens' work. What opinion could I have worth listening to! That there was no malice in him, no real vice. That it must have been simply that when he felt the pull against his collar it was some nameless abyss behind him, some unimaginable horror dragging him back, a fearful thing to be fought against with all the frenzied strength that was in him. Do you tell a farmer with muck on his boots that his horse is a wonder of creation, a creature of God, not a three-quarter-bred Fordson tractor? Was there indeed any degree of skill or forbearance that would serve any longer? Perhaps he'd already learned one thing too many; that he'd measured his strength against men and found that nothing could hold him.

As he lumbered into his stall, blowing at his manger, shaking himself like a half-drowned dog as I stripped off his harness, there was mercifully no voice to tell me that this was for the last time. But so it had been decided. There was nothing else for it. Chesterfield September Fair was only a week or two away, and so he was to be washed and combed and pampered and powdered this one last time.

And what a show he made! His coat shone like red silk, the ribbons I had plaited into his mane and tail streaming in the wind. There was pride to temper my sadness in my place at his head. The farmers and dealers looked him over and picked at the cobbles with their sticks, then looked again, eyed narrowed under their low-peaked caps, jaws set and sunk on their chests, faces closed in advance against the blandishments of the auctioneer.

"Gentlemen now, we have here the lot you've been waiting for. A rising four year-old gelding the property of a farmer well known to you all. Look at him gentlemen; he speaks for himself, as fine a specimen as it has been my privilege to put before you for years. I shall sell him as sound, but, mind you, unbroken to work"

It seemed half in a dream that I went through the routine of trotting back and forth, showing him off while the bidding went on, bluff shouts, sly winks, scraps of rural wit.

"Forty guineas now, forty I'm bid gentlemen - I shall sell him at forty - on my right for the last time at forty guineas I sell him - gone!"

The farmer came down. I never saw the face of the man who took the halter from my hand.

The end of the story too I never saw, except in my mind where I've pictured it a thousand times. They said this farmer had put him in a three-horse land-press that would break any horse down. Whether his whip was too keen or his feet too slow there was no-one to tell when they got him, out dead from under it. They would have stood there, in a half-circle about the horse, heavy-coated figures, shadows in the late October mist; and I can see him, head high, nostrils wide, eyes staring every muscle a-quiver, alone. My Captain!

And so at last the man came with the horse-box, and there, where he stood in the ring of shadowed faces, they shot him. Memories! Memory is a fickle thing and most things you forget in time, most places, even the voices and faces of those you have loved. But I'll never forget Captain.

Chapter 5
Leaving Farming Behind
-the Army-and marriage

Horses had sparked off my rather belated love affair with farming. For four years they had started my day at half-past five - in winter with the first feed of the day, and in summer with the walk down the Grey Banks with three or four lumps of sugar in those glorious early mornings of June, to call them up for the day's work. But the end was in sight for them. Captain's place was never filled. One empty stall, and there'd soon be more. And with their going some of the clouds of glory melted away. I was short of money too and got an itch in my heels. I could do two jobs. Quite a few of my late school friends I was now playing cricket and football with at the weekends worked in the local colliery offices, and quite on spec. I wrote asking for a job, and got it, Junior invoice clerk, twenty-five shillings a week. Not much, but the going rate at the time, and in addition I was making nearly a hundred a year out of pigs and doing enough general work at home to pay for my keep. George had left school, taking my place on the farm, and there was a feeling in the air that the worst of the Depression was over both in farming and in industry. Dad had changed the Morris Cowley tourer for a Rover Pilot twelve horse-power saloon and was thinking of buying a second tractor. Suddenly the pits were working four shifts and more, busier than they had been for years.

I fitted in very easily at Bolsover. Even where the older

staff were strangers, their names were familiar through sons and daughters and younger brothers I'd known at school. That rough youth Cosser Horden who'd been "Cock of the School" when I was eight, was this same smart chap in black jacket, striped trousers and Anthony Eden hat who worked opposite me now. It was a tight little community of conscientious hard workers. To say the least I was surprised when my first mornings work was flung back at me as being indecipherable. Here too, as at home, there was plenty of competition, in speed of work, accuracy of figures, in the pride of presentation of fine hand-written accounting books. I soon got the message; standards of writing and figures were far beyond any that my teachers had ever dreamt of. Well, second best had never been a comfortable position for me, so I learned afresh how to add up, and put my fountain pen away and learned to write all over again. I embarked on evening study for the exams of the Chartered Institute of Secretaries. All this concentration on getting through as much work as possible might be looked on rather cynically nowadays as a priggish attitude. Then, it was general, the common defence against unemployment; God would help those who helped themselves.

I got used for the first time to working with girls, in an atmosphere quite different from social meetings outside working hours. The free and easy daily contact was a new experience, quite outside the cloistered life behind the plough. There would be a couple of dozen of them, typists and comptometer operators, mostly under thirty as there was no question of continuing work after marriage. The married

Sergt. Cornelius Turner
Sherwood Foresters.
1939.

women at work were school teachers, shop workers and factory workers - near us, perhaps one woman in twenty. There were lots of office crushes and most of our girls married "into the office" after engagements lasting four or five years, to install themselves proudly in brand new semis at fifteen shillings a week mortgages. Hire purchase was unknown, you bought what you could pay for, and most couples I knew were quite comfortable. It would be twenty years before I first met a divorced person!

It was a time of heated politics and we argued endlessly. I switched opinions wherever the disagreement was sharpest, more for love of my own voice than any firm conviction. I was a true blue campaigning for a new trade union, and argued volubly for pacifism while I kept up my Yeomanry attendances at the Drill Hall. I gave up football for hockey as they had a good team at the office with a couple of county players. Evenings and Sundays were busy with swotting or farm work. Girls drifted in and out of my life and I went dancing regularly; the regular Saturday hops at the Church Hall cost a shilling while the smarter affairs - half-a-crown, dinner jacket jobs (Burton's made dinner jacket suits to measure for three guineas). By now I'd got myself a motor-bike again, a Sunbeam this time which meant I could always find a dancing partner but wasn't much of a marriage prospect.

I saw my cousins Mary and Kathy now and again. Uncle Bert had left Blackwell Church Farm and taken Springs Farm, Edingly, near Southwell and when I rode over now and again

Mary and Kathy were full of gossip about strange boyfriends. They worked in Nottingham now and seemed too grand for me. And then I heard that Mary had married a Nottingham bank clerk, and I was desolated. It wasn't long afterwards that I got engaged to the prettiest girl in Bolsover, Margery Crossland, whose father was head of the Orders department at the office. Sometimes twice a week in winter we would go dancing until gone two in the morning followed by bread and cheese and cocoa to warm us up for the cold ride home on the Sunbeam, Madge with her floor length dress pinned up round her waist. Often enough I've got home by four, then straight up to change into my farming clothes and down again to the stable to stretch out in a spare manger to doze until stables time. So passed those five years of my life as Invoice, Costing, Share Registration clerk cum student, cum farmer, cum political agitator.

If I'd had the gumption to realise it I was being passed from department to department for experience, getting more than my share of salary rises, with plenty of chances of promotion in the offing. In my own defence I might say it was an irksome job for young blood in stirring times. The Abdication had come and gone taking Mrs Simpson with it. Churchill's voice was thundering in the hills of the political wilderness. We were fighting in Palestine against the Jews and the Italians had trumped up a full-scale war against Abyssinia - Eden had resigned over the acquiescence of the Government. Hitler was spreading himself over Northern Europe and Mussolini over the South. There was a civil war in Spain where we could not make up our minds which side to support, though it has been fashionable ever since to pretend we were wholeheartedly on the side of the eventual losers. I was working on the idea of forming a clerical trade union, and managed to arrange for a meeting of the whole staff at the Colliery School where the project was to be discussed under guarantee by the senior clerks that no accounts would be passed to the Management. I was the principal and most enthusiastic speaker. I was also on the mat in the Secretary's office by half-past nine the following day, where he told me sadly that I did not seem to be cut out for clerical work and accepted my resignation with alacrity.

I was working my notice when Hitler marched into Czechoslovakia. And so goodbye Bolsover! I was assistant manager of Bourne's Flour and Stock Feed Mill at Clowne for three months and then off to camp with the Territorials in June and July for a month. Then, about 10.30 p.m. 21st August I came out of the cinema with Madge and there was Captain Houldsworth with orders for Lance-sergeant Turner to report to the Drill Hall the following morning. Madge and I had got rather a habit with each other and though we did not realise it then, when we parted that night, it was for good. We did not meet again until I ran into her in Mansfield six years later, looking a picture of health, a sight for sore eyes, with a fine three year old boy beside her. We had a cup of tea and toast and I have never seen her again.

A year or so before, I had listened to old Lord Baldwin at a Young Conservative rally. Some of his words ring still in my ears. "I have had my hour, and soon pass into the shade. But for you, life stretches before you like a boundless sea, and the imagination of youth is already launching flotillas of dream-ships upon its waters." And then I found myself putting on the rough khaki uniform with no thought but the morrow what years would pass by, what friends would come and go, what new horizons loom and fade away before I set it aside. Casually, quite unknowing, I said goodbye to Palterton too that night. I would go back from time to time, but merely as a visitor; those well-loved hills and fields would never be home to me again. The wide world beckoned my generation with the voice of the trumpet.

> Beyond the sound of the ebb and flow,
> Out of sight of lamp and star,
> It calls you where the good winds blow -
> Where the unchanging meadows are.
>
> From faded hopes and hopes agleam
> It calls you, calls you night and day,
> Out of the dark, into the dream,
> Over the hills and far away.

It was hot in the Drill Hall at Staveley and I was alone and sleepy on lunch-time telephone duty, the flies buzzing in the slant beams of the midday sun. The Sergeant-Major had nipped out for a quick one or two, and there were three or four of the officers across in the Mess as the tinkle of the set brought me up short. As I casually enquired what the message was, a snappy voice in no uncertain tone ordered me to take the message down:

PLUMER REQUIRES ALL POSTS TO BE MANNED IMMEDIATELY STOP FROM TROOPERS STOP TIME OF ORIGIN 1250 HRS 24 AUGUST 39 STOP

For a few seconds I stared at the message pad, only half believing, the hair rising at the back of my neck. Then I snatched it up and raced down the corridor, waving it like a standard, barging unchecked into the Mess. "It's here! It's here!!" I said. A tot of whisky was shoved into my hand, and champagne squirted round the walls as bedlam was let loose. What a time for Cousin Kathy's favourite recitation to go through my mind.

> And there was mounting in hot haste, the steed,
> The mustering squadron and the clattering car
> Went pouring forward with impetuous speed
> And swiftly forming into the ranks of war.

Out went the pre-arranged calls to the harvest fields, black coal-faces, steel furnaces, offices, shops, schools, factories, the bedrooms of shift workers, the dole queues, the street corners, the pigeon lofts and the pubs. Report to the Drill Hall, full uniform and equipment. By eight o'clock that night, approaching dusk, our three hundred and sixty men, twenty searchlights and sound locators, lorries, field kitchens, stores, clothing, bedding and rations were pulling to a standstill before our new home, an empty four acre paddock sixty miles away.

A whole world had passed us by in those few hours, it was a new beginning. What had gone would always be to us "Before the War!"

Our new home, this field beside the railway station at the pleasant little Yorkshire village of North Cave, a dozen miles west of Hull, soon began to have a lived-in look. The orderly lines of bell-tents looked smart in the sunshine. The company transport lines were neatly dressed off; latrines were dug in the far corner; the half dozen marquees for Company Office, Quartermaster Stores, Messes, Fitters and Red Cross and the guard on the gate gave the whole establishment a business-like look. The day after our arrival I had gone in Orders as Orderly Room Sergeant in charge of pay and administration - I was not long in adopting the traditional sergeant's opinion that the officers were there to do as they were instructed.

The first ten days we lived with one ear glued to the wireless, alternately high with excitement as war seemed possible or miserably downcast when it seemed Chamberlain would give way once more as he had done at Munich twelve months before. The villagers found the soldiers a novelty and they fixed up a dance for us on Saturday night in the village hall, there was a dimpled- cheeked brunette who caught my eye, and I danced with her all the evening. Her name was Grace. When I saw her home just after midnight, it was to the largest house in the village, the home of the local MP, she was Nanny to his grandchildren. It was already Sunday and ten hours later in the crowded mess we were listening to the quiet voice of

Chamberlain telling us the war had begun.

The wild celebrations that followed that Sunday gave way to anticlimax as nothing war-like happened. I got down to my job organising the pay. Sappers 2/- a day, Bombardiers 4/-, Sergeants 6/-, all wives 14/- a week, children 4/- a week for the first, 3/- the second, 2/- the third, 1/- a piece for any excess. Allotments had to be arranged so that the wives got their due. Half a married soldier's pay went directly to his family, so a soldier with three children got 7/- a week for himself while his wife had the other 7/-, plus her own 14/-, plus 9/- for the children, £1 10s in all for her and 7/- for him, a bit more than a farm labourer who got £1 15s in Derbyshire. The soldiers' 7/- would buy him eight pints of beer and four ounces of tobacco or sixty cigarettes. I had wangled the motorbike into the Hired Vehicles Pool, earning me a further 10/- a day so I was never badly off. Grace and I would go off to Hull or Beverley on her days off for an afternoon at the pictures, tea at a nice cafe, and home on the bike. I thought she'd soon got into the way of pillion riding but found that she'd already had quite a bit of practice. We saw each other most evenings as the autumn wore on. Back in September Madge had written breaking off our engagement, news I received with relief as Grace occupied more and more of my thoughts. We became engaged at Christmas. A bitterly cold winter it was with temperatures near zero Fahrenheit and we both learned to skate on the pond where the ice lay thick and unbroken until March.

And there is another little story there. It was just as cold in

France. Mother's oldest brother Bert, Mary's father, had been leader of that quartet of harum-scarum Yeomanry brothers who had ridden swanking off to that other war in August 1914. This new war stirred the blood of the old war-horse now nearer 60 than 50, and off went the ex-Sgt. Major veteran of Gallipoli and Salonika and talked his way into the King's Commission as a Lieutenant in the Pioneer Corps. By the time we had settled in at North Cave, Uncle Bert was in France, but however willing the spirit, it wouldn't last; that bitter winter saw through the old rogue and he was invalided out and packed off home. Later that summer Aunt Aggie, always my favourite aunt, showed me round the farmhouse, The Walnuts, Barnstone, and showed me cupboards full of Army blankets, boots, greatcoats, shirts and socks. It was like an Aladdin's Cave. "They'd have found the old devil out you know," she said fondly "They'd have court martialed him. He only got out just in time!"

I too had been put forward for a commission that first autumn but the crabby Border Regt. Brigadier who interviewed me was looking for farmers who rode horses rather than drove them so it was another whole year before I got my orders to report to Lichfield barracks on my way to Officer training Unit at Douglas on the Isle of Man.

Grace and I were married before I went. I got 48 hours leave; the 21st December was a bright clear day, sharp with frost which struck a ring out of the stone flags as my army Boots clumped down the aisle of Scarcliffe Church. Mary* was the

Corney and Grace
"Just Married"

only member of Grace's family there. Travelling was difficult and Jim* was in Gibraltar. He was on the Guardian, his two previous ships, the Glorious and the Gypsy having gone to the bottom of the Med. We spent our wedding night at Bassett Farm, Langwith, and that night the Germans dropped the only local bomb of the war, not half a mile away.

*Mary and Jim were Grace's Sister and brother

By April 1941 I was installed as a brand new second Lieutenant in a barbed wire compound on the beach at Skegness commanding a platoon of the Sherwood Foresters with one brick and concrete pill-box, one Lewis machine gun, one sawn-off naval quick-firing six-pounder and thirty men with rifles and five bullets each, defending the shores of England. "Halt! Who goes there!" sang out my sentry, one night he thought he saw some movement behind the wire, and feeling I am sure, slightly ridiculous with the time-honoured challenge. The prompt reply was a bullet past his ear. When he'd got his face out of the sand we got the whole Lincolnshire Army out of bed - but we never found the shooter. It was the nearest we'd been to the war. By July we were on aerodrome defence at Binbrook near Louth. Living and messing on a permanent operational RAF station was luxury after the blankets in the sand dunes at Skegness. Army life seemed very tame compared with all this; every night the Wellingtons were rumbling off towards Germany or the Channel ports, and although there were daily gaps in the Mess, in no time at all I found myself putting in for transfer to RAF air-crew.

I begged rides on the daily test-flights, nominally to see air how our camouflage looked from the air.

Tony Bracchi had arrived soon after me at Binbrook. We were much a contrasting pair it was strange how firm our friendship became. He was a tall reedy fellow, several years my junior, expensively educated, and quite impractical as a soldier. All the same, his drawling cultivated voice and a natural assumption of authority went down to a tee with his platoon. He himself had scant respect for authority or superior rank, and posed as an ardent socialist; I thought him a bit of a dreamer. But for the first time in his company I began to doubt much of what I had been taught in the name of education. He talked easily about the London stage while I had never been inside a theatre; he had a couple of records of Schubert's Unfinished Symphony that I used to put on his portable gramophone when he was out, and I don't think he ever guessed that it was the very first piece of classical music I learned to know. For his part he seemed fascinated by my knowledge of weapons and how to use them and about soldiering generally and the way I was 'at home' in the country. I certainly felt a proper bumpkin when he took me up to London for a weekend. His parents lived in a very smart flat in Chesham Square only a few yards from the walls of Buckingham Palace gardens, and he showed me round night-time Piccadilly and Leicester Square and the dives and naughty girls of Greek Street with the air of a proprietor. I got him out of one or two scrapes with the C.O. and helped him with his platoon when he got in a fix. Left to himself he would quite easily have got lost when out of sight of the airfield. And in return he taught me the difference between Kummel and Grand Marnier.

That winter of 1941/42 was another severe one and I managed to catch pneumonia, spending five weeks in hospital at Bracebridge, coming out with the bluebells to find our company transferred to a Fighter airfield at Kirton-Lindsay. Tony took me round the three squadrons one RAF, one Polish RAF, and one American RAF. The polish 303 Squadron was full of much-decorated mad-men who'd already made a famous name for themselves at Biggin Hill in the Battle of Britain. The Americans were freelance volunteer barnstorming pilots in search of a war and called themselves the Eagle Squadron. It was our first contact with the Yanks, and, since Pearl Harbour had just brought their country into the war, they were soon joined by the first units of the U.S.A.A.F. with their beautiful twin boom P38 Pursuit Fighters. Their most distinguished pilot was Captain Clark Gable, getting on for 40 by then and looked on as a sort of uncle by the other pilots. He lived a quieter life than most in the Mess, not at all in the hellraiser mould of the rest of the Americans and the Poles!

My transfer request had been practically forgotten when we suddenly heard that a glider unit was being formed to compliment the Parachute Regiment which was in its infancy. The Germans had just swept us out of Cyprus, using gliders for the first time and with great success, and the brass-hats had now decided to copy them, and were building gliders big enough to carry a jeep and tractor, or a jeep and light field gun or around 40 men. Tony and I found our names had been transferred willy-nilly from our RAF aircrew request to this brand new unit and in no time we were reporting to RAF Cardington for our medical. I had the wind up about this for two reasons, first I'd only recently recovered from a bad dose of pneumonia and secondly my old deafness was always at the back of my mind although it had never reoccurred after my operation of ten years back. However, I had become a bit of a fitness fanatic: I was in the regimental boxing and cross-country teams and my platoon had just won a local Army Run-March trophy. The medical turned out, in the jargon of the day, a piece of cake. I guess they were passing everybody just then.

Alan was born at Palterton 19th August, the day after Grace's 30th birthday and I got a 48 hour leave-pass. Grace and son seemed reasonably well and I suppose she was relieved that I was still safely tucked away in the wilds of North Lincolnshire. However, on my return, orders to report to Glider Pilot Training H.Q., Tilshead, Salisbury Plain, awaited me, and before the day was out Tony and I were saying goodbye to the Foresters and setting off for the South.

Then began a training period tougher that anything we'd ever seen, all new-comers without regard to rank were squadded for six weeks barrack square training under drill sergeants brought in from the Guards H.Q. at Caterham. It was purgatory! I'm afraid it was not quite Tony's cup of tea: the battering of the drill sergeants was more than he could tolerate and back he went to Lincolnshire, while I went off to Elementary Flying

Training School with my brand new Army Air Corps badge and red beret. That autumn we spent learning to fly Tiger Moths, the old fashioned box-kite biplanes, the primary trainers for all aircrew. And now at last I knew I had found what I'd been looking for. I enjoyed every minute. Captain "Bunny" Hare beat me by half an hour in the race for First Solo which I passed with flying colours. Squadron Leader Bert Tribe, Chief Flying Instructor, had one comment to make "Not bad at all. You'll do. But there's one thing and remember, I'm never wrong. You're too cocky and one day you will crash. All the best!" and he stomped off to Flying Control to watch my next take-off. After that, Bunny and I daily followed each other round the sky trying mock fights and new stunts for hour after hour until we were thoroughly at home and at ease in the air. After Christmas we transferred to gliders at Brize Norton. If anything I found gliders even more to my liking: I never had a moment's anxiety and in March 1943 I received my Wings at the passing out parade before the King at Parkhill.

It's perhaps interesting to know what happened to the fifteen officers who had started the course the previous August. Eight (of whom Tony Bracchi was one) were sent back to their units, and one crashed and 'went for a burton'. Of the six who passed out three were killed in our first operation, the Sicily landing, and one at Arnhem. Bunny Hare who became Squadron Commander was kicked out of the regiment in Africa for criticising the Sicily operation. So I was the one left to be demobbed in one piece at the end of the war. May found us bound for Africa and just outside Philipville, at a base-camp there, I ran into Private Swallow whom I'd left behind in Lincolnshire. All the Foresters at Kirton Lindsay had been transferred to the 1st Battalion which had been practically wiped out at Tobruk. They had got to Africa ahead of me after all and straight away ran into a fearful pasting at a place called Green Hill outside Medfez-el-Bab in Tunisia, not far from the site of ancient Carthage. Swallow told me my old colleagues Capt. Jimmy Molloy and Lieut. Bracchi had both been killed. Poor Tony. "We had this order to advance" he said, "and Mr Bracchi just stood up and walked straight forward across this bare hillside, swinging his walking-stick the way he always did. They cut us to ribbons!" About 21st April, must have been St. George's Day or thereabouts. He was a good friend, and even forty years on I still see him in my mind whenever I drink a Grand Marnier.

Chapter 6
To North Africa and Sicily
Plus meeting Tito

The war in North Africa was over by the time we reached Tunisia and set up camp on the desert air-strips outside the walls of the Holy City of Kairiouan. These airstrips made up a whole region of dead flat burning dry salt pans, endlessly edged in shimmering mirage, were our base for the forthcoming Sicily landing. The invasion of Europe, no less, was to be our regimental overture though we did not know it yet. I'd better say a word about our gliders. Our British machine was called a Horsa; it was a hefty aircraft, made entirely of wood with a plywood skin, about 80 feet in length and width, the body a 10 feet diameter cylinder. It was strong and could take a pretty hard crash and if empty would float in water for a long time. It carried a load of 7000lbs, but it was a clumsy brute and hard work for the C47 American transport planes (the RAF called them Dakotas) that towed us. However we'd only got a fraction so far of the two hundred gliders we should need, so we had to learn to fly the American Wacos which were being assembled in good numbers at Casablanca. The Waco was much smaller and more fragile. The body was a light alloy tubular framework with a canvas skin. It carried 4000lbs, did not float, but was much easier to fly both for glider pilot and the tow-ship, provided we did not fly through the heat of the day, over 120 °F?, when the turbulence was terrific at the comparatively low heights at which we flew. We lost one Waco and all its occupants over Relizane in Algeria: it

Corney on Active Service
in North Africa 1943.

just blew apart in mid air. So our flying was confined to the hours of 05.00 to 10.00 and 18.00 hrs until morning. There was something quite unforgettable about the evening and night flying over the southern desert. The indescribable sunsets, the limitless visibility after the wind and the heat died down, the walled Holy City 5000 feet below, over which we seemed to hang motionless, as the last of the sun, swiftly dipping to the horizon, shot with gleams of gold and silver the toy-like mosques and minarets of the ancient town. A half forgotten song of school days ran over and over in my mind:

> There is no solace on earth for us or such as we
> Who search for the hidden beauties that eyes may never see
> We travel the dusty road till the light of day is dim
> And the sunset shows us spires away on the world's rim.
> Not for us are content, and quiet and peace of mind,
> For we go seeking cities that we may never find.

Back to training! We were doing night landings, the tow-ships taking us say 10 miles from our L.Z. (landing zones) to which we would fly in free flight on a known compass bearing, hoping we got back to the right place. What we called a 'remote release'. And when we hit the target after a lovely flight over the desert, bright as day under the desert moon, we thought we had it licked. As it turned out that night of 9 July 1943 off Syracuse it was a slaughter of the innocents! Out of 140 gliders leaving Africa, two of them made pin-point landings beside the Bridge which was our primary target. Another dozen were somewhere near. And these two captured the Bridge, then lost it, then recaptured it helped by the Eighth Army who made sea-borne landings.

Instead of limitless flat sand the landing area was rocky deeply ravined country, such as millions of holiday makers have since seen on almost any Mediterranean coast. No-one seemed to have realised how nearly impossible the task was. And in place of the African moon there was anti-aircraft fire. Instead of a known "casting-off" point, the tow-ships had only the sea below them with the phosphorescence of the breakers on the shore making it hard to judge the distance between one mile and ten! There just had been no realistic training for either glider pilots or tow-ship pilots. In the sea and on the land we lost over a quarter of our 280 pilots in the first three hours of our first operation. Incidentally, no glider-pilot ever wore a parachute; when your glider went down, you went down with it!

Who me? Oh yes, well I had all this from hearsay. That is to say I wasn't actually on the spot. In my Waco glider I had a round dozen men with some 3" mortars and ammunition to make up the weight. A mortar is a kind of portable gun that fires a very high trajectory shell with obvious uses in badly broken ground, rocky terrain or built-up areas. It was quite dark as we took of about 20.00 hrs without incident. Our tow-ship did a bit of dodging about, perhaps looking for other planes. If so he would be disappointed for from the moment to take-off we never saw anyone else in the air. We cleared the coast over Sousse about 21.00 hrs, the breakers clearly visible, the sea an

THE AMERICAN WACO GLIDER

invisible black void. As we got our night vision, the dark silhouette of the C47, hanging steadily in position ahead and slightly below, was clearly outlined so that in the clear air did not need the navigation lights on his tail and wing tips. I thought we had a glimpse of Malta, more or less on track after an hour but couldn't be sure. The intercom, which was a telephone line through the tow-rope to the tow-ship, had as usual gone u/s on take-off. By now there was a cloud wrack thickening under a sky lightened by an invisible moon and we were glad of the position lights as we met wisps of cloud. We climbed and climbed, much higher than the planned height, and began to feel the cold. For a time there was a pattern of tracer bullets far below then the light cloud again. We were supposed to have flown approximately NE from Sousse bringing us to the right of the southern extremity of Sicily then come in with a left hook on to the coast at Syracuse, at 3000 feet. But we were wheeling about the sky in all directions and at 8000 feet! Most of us had never been as high! I had the feeling that we were over land, and when at last I saw the C47 waggle its wings I took a deep breath and told Sergeant "Droop" Newman to let the rope go.

We were on our own, quiet now, our speed having dropped from 130 mph to 70, as we gradually sank into the murk below, hoping to see the ground before it saw us. Not a sign of life. Then Newman thought there was a hillside on our left and suddenly there it was, just a second or two to realise that the great black bulk was not a cloud but a mountainside. Touch and bounce - hit the wing - slew round - crash and bounce again - lose everything, head down, arms round drawn up knees, the last long scraping crash and silence. Good old Bert Tribe, he was right! He was not wrong. As I started gently to uncoil myself someone put a boot on my face. No-one was screaming. There was a burst of quiet intensive swearing and I recognised the voice of the mortar platoon sergeant. Someone had a torch. "Keep that torch down!", " Which way is down Sarge?" Somebody giggled a bit hysterically.

There were various aches and pains but not a broken bone between us. One wing had disappeared, the other pointed at the moon, now racing helter-skelter through the clouds.

In the early morning we found the pieces littering the mountainside, plywood and canvas blowing in tattered strips in the wind. Someone had found a hollow among the rocks to make a fire and we had a brew-up which became a proper bacon and biscuit fry, as one of the guards we'd put out homed accurately on the smell of breakfast, prodding two black-coated Italians in front of him, with three or four bare-foot children, thumb-sucking and wide-eyed, trailing behind. It transpired we were somewhere on the slopes of Mount Etna - the altimeter read nearly four thousand feet. Catania was somewhere in the mists below us, as was the Herman Goering Division of the German Army! We had fetched up about 60 miles from target.

Soon a few more of the locals turned up, men and women in penny numbers, the women bartering water for cigarettes and the children happily giving a hand to collect brushwood to pile on our wreck for camouflage. We were sure they would give us away and there was nothing we could do about it, but no Germans came. When we made as if to do a reconnaissance down the hill the Italians dissuaded us. "No, no! Tedesci boom boom !" they pantomimed out rifle fire, pointing down towards the distant city, while the tattered children mingled happily amongst us, showing no fear of these strange creatures who had tumbled like fallen angels out of the midnight sky. And so we remained, sitting out this little piece of the war with them, until after fourteen days the whole little community came excitedly over. "Guerra finira" they said "Tedesci kaput!" they laughed and slapped their thighs, as we shook hands all round, gave them the last of our cigarettes, and followed them down the mountain. Two days later we landed, all present and correct at Bizerta.

The general licking of wounds was still going on. Some of the lads were stitching new medal ribbons on to their uniforms and looking suitably modest. Sergeant Major Wally Masson, who already had a Military Medal, now had a D.F.M. to go with it. He also got a direct commission and came to our squadron as a brand new Second Lieutenant. But there'll be more of Wally later. There was an undercurrent of revolution about. Colonel George Chatterton had not come out at all well out of Operation Husky. He had got a new rank of Brigadier and a nice medal, although he had landed in the sea. I sided firmly with the critics but he was sharp and decisive enough to sack his two senior plotters at an hour's notice. Major Bunny Hare was one of them, and I counted myself lucky not to be sacked with him. He was the best squadron commander I ever had.

New plans were afoot. Italy was due to be invaded and our training on the desert strips took up where we had left off for Operation Husky, and just then an unforgettable character briefly crossed my path. Major Peniakov, known throughout the Desert as Popski, was creator and leader and paymaster of Popski's Private Army, a tiny mob of iron hard men, already legendary from Cairo to Tunis. They were made up of his Polish countrymen. Desperadoes all, a selection of the elite Long Range Desert Group, the new Special Air Service and, so it was said, a couple of deserters from the Africa Corps and the Foreign Legion. Popski was a man born to fight, born to lead, like Bader and Stirling, the German Skoszeny and the Irishman Paddy Mayne, Vic Cocon of the Parachute Regt., and Wingate of the Chindits, men who carried with them an aura of magnetism and a degree of personal courage that could only be manifest in war. They were an inspiration to all who knew them. Popski was not the least of them.

He had fitted out a dozen or so Jeeps, armed to the teeth, machine guns mounted front and rear, crewed by this international land of cut-throats. With the desert war at an end Popski looked about him for the quickest way into Europe and hit upon gliders. He'd sworn to be first to Rome and gliders would carry his Jeeps most of the way there. I was to fly him about the night sky of Tunisia to show him the flying performance and the load-carrying capacity while he thought out various navigation and pin-point landing exercises. One night we had done a "remote release" and let the tow-ship go some twelve or fifteen miles back and glided in freely to try to pin-point the landing zone in the dark. I was describing the last stages of the landing to him as he stood between the pilot's seats. My second pilot Sgt. Hutson, who was doing the flying, got a shade low on the down wind leg, and turning in to land in a vertical bank, bounced the wing-tip on the deck, recovered, and made some sort of landing, while Popski raised one eyebrow but continued smoking his cigar. When we got out we found half the wing was gone at which he roared with laughter and thought it an excellent demonstration of the Waco.

I was disappointed when the powers that be turned down Popski's plan (though I do believe he might have got me into, mischief in the end). As it happened we went into Taranto by sea, about 1 September 1943 on the Dutch destroyer Beatrice, but no sooner did we reach dockside than Popski was away over the hill with his three Jeeps. Rome was 250 miles away and it was eight months later before we marched into the Eternal City. But Popski was back in ten days, having motored 500 miles through the enemy lines to Rome and back. His men had over-painted the "Popski's Private Army" signs on the Jeeps to read "Pope Pius' Angels". A year later he left an arm on the Greek island of Cos but otherwise finished the war intact, looking with his iron hook like Long John Silver brought to life. You couldn't say he was a man in a million - his sort are thinner on the ground than that.

After the landing the war got away to the northward and by December the front line stretched across the country just north

of Naples, the 8th Army in the river Sangro in the right flank and the American 5th Army on the left along the rivers Volturno and Garigliano and a bitter winter for all it was. South of Naples and way from the ports of Taranto, Salerno and
Bari Calabria was a mountainous, hungry, primitive country with no income but the sparse produce of the soil. The little white towns inland had been bypassed by the war. Set on their hilltops, the cobbled town square surrounded by a warren of narrow streets of box shaped houses bleached by the sun, they were desperately poor. Until a few weeks ago they had been our enemies but it was impossible to feel anything but pity for them as our trucks and Jeeps pushed their creaking carts into the gutter and our troops strode arrogantly through their midst scarce condescending to acknowledge their existence. And yet, in the quiet of the evening, with a few young folk parading the town, the old men smoking over their glasses of wine in the square, the women plying their needles, gossiping quietly in front of their houses, the church bell tolling, the priest hurrying along on some errand of comfort, a girl leaving a few wild flowers at a wayside shrine, well, then you did sometimes have time to ponder just what were these gifts of freedom, civilisation and progress we, the conquerors, were bringing into their way of life.

In November the 1st Airborne Division went home, except for a third of the Parachutists and one squadron of gliders. Ours! We were here to stay in the Med. apparently for the duration. We were at a little town called Putignano, not far from Bari, and I discovered a little clothing factory there. I had the notion of sending home a hat and coat rig-out for Alan and when I made them understand my idea, all the women crowded round to put in their suggestions for "Il bambino inglesi." And so in a day or two they produced a nice little sky-blue overcoat with matching hat trimmed with blue rabbit fur, which eventually arrived safely at Palterton, his first present from Santa Claus.

By early December we were flying back to North Africa to Oudfda a desert airstrip in French Morocco. Oudfda was Foreign Legion country midway between Fez and Sidi-bel-Abbes, 2000 feet up in the foothills of the Atlas, where Africa can be pretty cold at night and we had a solid cover of snow for Christmas. It was pretty comfortless in the stark red sand stone foreign legion barracks, unfurnished, unheated, dust-floored, just the bare stone walls and doors and wooden shutters over the unglazed window apertures. We were in the command of the American Air Corps. Waco gliders were arriving in crates at Casablanca by the hundred and here started our steady job of fully testing and ferrying them airborne across the Med.; by the following July we had delivered 600 Wacos to the Rome area without a single human casualty, although tow-rope failures lost us around a dozen gliders, some of them in the sea. There were of course quite a few write-offs during testing but we managed to walk away from them all.

With Christmas coming up, Oudfda was turning out to be a dry station. Because we were darting about back and forth across North Africa our normal whisky and cigarette rations had not caught up with us so something had to be done and this is where Wally Masson had his great idea. Wally had joined the Argyle and Southern Highlanders about 1933 and got himself drafted to the India station. Coming home after four years away in 1937 they had instead been put off at Gibraltar on account of the Civil War brewing up across the border in Spain. Now in a boring place like Gib. it was only natural that there should be nightly outbreaks of fisticuffs between the Army and Navy garrisons in the dance-halls of the little town, and Wally, by now Army fly-weight and bantam-weight boxing champion was foremost in the fight. Well Wally reckoned that Gib. was swimming in booze if only there were some way to get at it. We consulted a couple of the Yanks who were, if anything, more thirsty than we were, and with them we concocted this training exercise. We would fly a train (tow-ship and glider) to Casablanca on a routine training run. The tow-ship would have engine trouble and divert to the northward. Then, over the Straits, the engine trouble would become acute and the pilot would have no alternative to cast us off near Gib., leaving us to make our landing there, and he would come in behind us. While they put their engine to right, Wally, with pockets full of dollars led us off to find the drinks!

For a time all went as planned; I piloted the glider with Wally as co-pilot behind a plane-load of thirsty C47 pilots. They turned out a smart staff car to pick us up on landing and in no time at all we were whisked through a dark arched entrance inscribed in stone: Fortress Headquarters. Before we could offer our thanks to our hosts in a civilised way we were abruptly told we were under arrest. Our cover story did not

make any impression.
We had:

(1) Deserted from the British North Africa theatre of war
(2) Landed at a forbidden airfield
(3) Taken part in unauthorised use of British and American Military aircraft
(4) Generally laid ourselves open on half-a-dozen counts Chargeable at a Field General Court Martial.

This was not funny so we abandoned our story and came clean with the Fortress Commander. We were an inoffensive bunch of idiots, our wits addled by the scorching desert suns, our throats parched by the searing Khamsin winds blowing out of the burning heart of the Black Continent.

"Well, why didn't you say so in the first place?" He had his eyes on Wally's medal ribbons and he could be softening. "You can't go landing anywhere just because you're thirsty!" He paused and ducked his head, with a swift glance over his shoulder.

"Nobody can land here! Tomorrow," he dropped his voice, "Tomorrow we are expecting a Very Important Personage, I shall let you go tomorrow morning on condition your C47 miraculously cures itself and disappears complete with glider by 14.00 hours."

It was an experience anyway. Not everybody has spent a night under arrest in the bowels of the Rock. In the morning they gave us an address and a chit to a Navy canteen store, and we walked out once more to the lovely freedom of the open air. Just off the main street Wally led us to a large bare hall smelling of stale beer. At the far end on either wing stairs slanted up to a low bandstand dais. This was where it all happened, six years back, the Navy defending the bandstand, the Army attacking, or vice versa, every night, twice nightly. As Wally finished this unlikely tale, a door opened and an enormous Spaniard waddled out to tell us the place was closed. Then he stopped dead, staring hard at Wally, came forward a step or two and flung out his arms.
"El Tigre! You come back El Tigre!" he shouted burying Wally in a great bear-hug. "Mamma mia, El Tigre", he held Wally off and gave him a mock right hook, taking in Wally's medalled tunic, "You fine officer now" he stepped back and letting his arms fall; "El Tigre!"

Our search was over. An hour later half a dozen small boys led the way down to the airfield bowed down with whisky, gin and cigarettes. We lined up at the extreme end of the tiny runway, pointing our nose at Africa, and Gib watched its one and only glider take-off of the whole war. We did a circuit to starboard round the Rock, giving a waggle of our wings as we came round low over the runway and headed south towards the dim rocky lagoon.

In the two hours flight back to Oudfda, Wally told us how, in

1938, bored with Gib., he'd been persuaded to "jump the fence" into Spain to join General Franco on the Ebro where the real fighting was. Returning to Blighty in 1939 he had been promptly court-martialled for desertion and sentenced to three years in the Glasshouse. Come the outbreak of war in September, they threw him out and back into the Highland Division as a private soldier. He'd got to be a sergeant again by the time the Highland Div. was captured in June 1940 at St. Valery. He escaped on the march and walked to the Swiss border only to be recaptured and taken to a POW camp in Silesia on the Polish border. It took him most of two years to escape again and make his way from Silesia to Madrid picking up several companions on the way. They gave him his Military Medal and he came to the Glider Pilot Regiment as Company Sergeant Major. A year later he took a leading part in the capture of the Bridge at Syracuse before being taken prisoner by the Italians. However he was not an easy man to keep down. With his knowledge of Spanish he was able to persuade the Italian Commandant that the British "Red Devils", even then coming off the beaches, took no prisoners, and his best course of action under promise of safe-conduct, was to surrender his garrison of a hundred men to Wally and march down to the beach. They recommended him for a D.C.M. By mistake it came through as a Distinguished Flying Medal, and Wally got his direct commission in the field and came to our squadron, the only man I ever heard of to be commissioned in the British Army after doing time for desertion out of it. As the Americans used to say, he was something else again!

Early in the New Year we flew back to Sicily to a real aerodrome at Comiso and took up our training in co-operation with the Pathfinder Company of the 2nd Para. secret 'homing' devices they were testing; their operational role was to drop a day or so ahead of the main body which they would 'home' on to the correct dropping zone. Captain Peter Baker was their C.O. and we enjoyed working with him and also with his 2nd in command Dumbo Willans. Dumbo had knocked around the world a bit, starting off as an Australian cowboy having run away from home at sixteen. He was the fastest man I ever saw with a Colt 45 revolver - he would hold a handkerchief in his right hand at arms length in front of him then let it go, drawing and firing his gun, and catching the handkerchief about waist height at the same time on his gun barrel. He knew scores of cowboy songs and was a grand entertainer with his guitar. After the war he joined Irvings as a professional parachutist and broke several world jumping records. He married Mary Grant a well-known agony columnist on one of the women's' weeklies. Wally and I spent hours with him practising revolver shooting. Peter Baker at the end of the war went back to run the large family department store at St. Helier, Jersey, and I believe he is there yet.

Towards the end of January there were whispers of a new operation for which we might need Horsa gliders. We had Brigade; who were all experts equipped with various ones, but we heard of three which had been left on an airstrip in Tunisia after the Sicily job, and Major Robbie Coulthard, and our CO, sent me over with half a dozen pilots to have a look at them. The night before, I'd been over to see Bill Needle the Yank executive officer, and within a couple of hours he had three crews laid on for us, asked me to draw a pencil ring on the map and said sure they'd find them, he'd come over himself for the ride. Without labouring the point it did show up the difference between the RAF and the USAAF. It would have taken the RAF a week or ten days with every possible snag thrown in our way. It's an attitude all too common over the years; the English disease is a very real thing.

Well, we found them, looking very lonesome and forlorn out there in the salt flats. A little RAF detachment had trucked in from Algiers and the Sergeant fitter thought they'd be OK once we shovelled them clear of sand. Nothing seemed to be hanging loose, so we plugged in the tow-ropes and took off on a wing and a prayer and flew them straight across the Med. to Sicily. Back at Comiso we did some more testing and set out, fully loaded to fly to Bari where I heard I was to lead a flight of three gliders flying a Russian General Staff into Yugoslavia. Now we'd had a very difficult trip up from Sicily into a Northeast blizzard and it had taken four hours instead of two. There was no way we could expect to get Horsas to 7000 feet to cross the Dinaric Alps into the interior, so we agreed with the Yanks to switch to Wacos.

The brief was to deliver about 36 Russian officers under a Marshall Korneyev to a point on a mountainside called Medenapolu two kilometres NW of the town of Basan Petrovac 100 miles inland of the Yugoslav port of Split. It was to be in broad daylight (for the first time with gliders) and we would have 24 Spitfires outward escort over the sea, then 24 Mustangs taking over on the other side up to the target L.Z. There were also 50 Flying Fortress bombers carrying out a diversion raid in Zagreb!

Grace was expecting Christopher, in fact he was already born, but unbeknown as yet to me, so I could only write that I was off into the blue. I couldn't say where, I did not know when I should be back I would not be able to write and her letters would have to await my return.

My tow-ship pilot, Wendell C. Little of Indianapolis (he wrote it down on the back fly-leaf of my Bible) wished me luck just before take-off. "You'll need it" he said, "It's all over town this secret of yours; I hope they don't jump us." And so Operation Bunghole took off towards noon of a glorious clear day 19 February 1944, course approx. true north, visibility unlimited. As we neared landfall, scattered white islands in a black sea, we could already see the towering saw-tooth horizon of the mountains still sixty miles away. A town and harbour, that would be Split, dead on course. Droop Newman and I hardly said a word. He was doing the flying while I passed him a word now and again checking on course. The Marshall sat behind me, the muzzle of his machine pistol nestling about six inches from the back of my neck. As we approached the peaks Droop had all his work cut out to hold the rocking bucketing glider. I reckoned we were drifting east of track by several miles as we staggered over the divide the tow-ships and gliders leaping all over the sky. We tumbled over the icy teeth of the ridge with a hundred feet to spare.

The interior opened up before us, a great white valley, timbered on the high slopes and beyond the forests gentle hills losing themselves into the northern mists. Our dead reckoning time was up and there coming up below was the first town we had seen, not easy to pick out in the dazzling carpet of snow, but two miles to our left instead of to the right. We were east of track as I'd thought and flying straight on. Dare I pull off? I was certain I was right but there's no going back once you're off tow. I'd checked the map every mile of the way. No! This was not going to be another Etna. We'd got 3000 feet and could reach the L.Z. easily. "I'll take her Droop! Hit the tit! We're going down." He held up his hands then hit the release lever without a word. I pulled up the nose to get the speed down to 70, swinging to port as the rest of them flew straight on below me. Yes, this must be Petrovac, the L.Z. four or five miles away dead ahead now. "They're coming round" Droop shouted. The train had gone straight on for a couple of miles but were swinging round well above me now and overtaking fast. There was a wide white shelf on the hillside and a fire surely. Yes, a fire, two fires, little black dots against the snow. We were there! And then flashing past us came the Mustangs doing a mock beat-up. The others were off by now drifting gently down beside us, and we flopped down into three feet of snow. Three perfect landings.

Everybody embraced everybody else; the Partisans (Drugs they called themselves) armed to the teeth, rifles, crossed bandoliers, knives and grenades, bearded and stinking they swarmed over us. Anchoring the gliders down with fallen timber, we climbed on to the sleds and set off for town, the ponies up to their bellies in the track. It was a heavy night in the little town hall, as from six to near midnight we sat and drank toasts to the whole free world. "My government will not forget you and your pilots" someone was translating, "Tomorrow we meet our honoured leader Tito - he will regret he was not here this day" and so on until we all fell asleep about the floor.

The following day we looked around the town of maybe 5000 souls. It had a sort of primitive Tirolean character, the houses in natural unpainted timber, roofs of shingles or corrugated iron. A couple of iron minaret towers reminded us that the older inhabitants had been Turkish subjects. There were no shops, nothing to sell, rations of meat, potatoes and flour were daily distributed. Milk was for children only. There was no cheese, no beer, no wine, no tea, coffee or cocoa, no salt or yeast, no fruit, no lard, no butter to be found. Every meal, three good meals a day, was a bowl of steak and turnip soup with unleavened dry bread and water. The source of the steak could be anything on four legs and for five weeks we kept very fit on it though the water wore us down a bit. There were a few carts in the town, but no transport or access beyond the edge of town except by pack animals, ponies, mules or on foot.

Our sergeants McCulloch, Newman, Morrison, Hill and

McMillan were billeted together at the northern edge of the town and I was just across the road with three other officers who were part of the resident Military Mission. They had a sergeant and half a dozen signallers not far away, and elsewhere the Yanks had a Colonel with enough staff for two good poker schools. These missions had real jobs besides bridge and poker - the collection of baled-out aircrews and liaison with Cairo and Bari to arrange arms drops and such. Night after night we would lie out in the hillside, curled up in holes we'd dug to get out of the bitter winds, our straw fires laid out beside us, the signallers trying to make their homing beacons work. If we heard the unmistakable drone of the C47s we would race to put a light to them, to show the recognition code letter of the day. A couple of times there were men on the parachutes. They stayed a day collecting a guide and pack animal, then disappeared into the forest bound for Greece, Romania, Hungary or Austria to live out a hazardous and lonely war in some outpost of resistance.

In the first week we had the glider incident. There'd been a daily machine-gunning by patrolling J.U.88s and I got together with the local Drugs and arranged for them to provide ponies to pull the gliders into the forest edge where they could be more thoroughly hidden from the air. Besides, we'd heard at our briefing that the Krauts had some gliders of their own 50 miles away at Bihac, and with ours standing out on the snow like a sore thumb they might be tempted to start something. OK said the Drugs. Ponies come tomorrow said their interpreter. But of course they didn't. It was the usual Latin "Manana." Having been met with stupid grins instead of ponies for several days, I grew steadily more purple in the face. Our own people were just as amused and that didn't help. "You'll be lucky" said they. Well we'd see. The next morning I went down with Sgt. Hill and saw the local Commandant, and I deliberately and clearly let him know that if the gliders were not moved by midday following I would set fire to them. "OK," he said. "Ponies come!"

It was a glorious morning as Sgt Hill and I plodded out to the L.Z., and there the gliders lay just as they had landed. A bunch of Drugs supposedly guarding them sat round the fire just inside the tree line. Claude must have thought I looked a bit grim. "Can we really do it?" he asked, but I was already tearing the flying instruments out and stabbing at the canvas with Claude's knife and holding a match against the frayed ends. For a few seconds there was not enough smoke for the Drugs to notice from their fireside. Then in a bluster of wind the fire jumped the length of the fuselage, and as the Drugs ploughed through the snow towards us it was just a matter of standing back from the heat. While they were shouting and arguing among themselves, I turned to Claude, "Come on!" and started towards the next glider. The argument dissolved into silence for a moment, then pandemonium broke loose. "No, no, no!" they yelled. "We get ponies!" One or two rifles went off presumably into the air; "Ponies come now" they said, barring our way. In fact they were standing there all the time, harnessed to the Drugs sleighs, and in half an hour, before the ashes of my glider were cold, the other two were safely tucked away among the trees. As I felt the ashes, I thought of the men who had sweated to make my glider in Texas and Oregon, the GI's who had put it together at Casablanca, how we had flown it across deserts, seas and mountains, sun and blizzard a thousand miles and more. We didn't have much to say as we trudged home, Claude carrying the instruments, I still cooling off.

No-one else said much. The Drugs stepped back a bit, out of our way. Our own flock looked a bit keenly at me and stayed out of it. I think I must risk boring you with a word or two about guerrilla warfare, about Partisans. Churchill had said we would fight in the beaches and streets, in the fields and the hills - fine words but I'm glad it was never necessary. The serials on the telly, tell brave tales of the intrepid local school-masters and grocers, risking their all for love of country and no doubt many did and are still doing, somewhere. But real guerrilla warfare is not so simple. When gold, your actual golden sovereigns, start falling out of the sky, closely followed by rifles, grenades and the honeyed praises of idiotic liberal politicians, what else could possibly happen but that every cheap racketeer, every bully, everyone with a score to settle, every layabout slob will suddenly sit up and look smartly round for a piece of the action. In Yugoslavia as in France, Italy and Greece, the scum of the earth rose readily to the surface.

Many of the Drugs were just playing at soldiers. Not to overstate the case against them, they were tough and fit, able to do a good boy-scout act in their forests. If they were hungry they only had to kick down the door of some isolated cottage where some terrified woman would give them all the food she had. Then as now, the silly young girls were hanging round the necks of their cardboard heroes. But, as in all countries, there were many sterling characters, and the country was by a miracle granted an inspiring leader, perhaps the greatest leader and the most perceptive politician in Europe. Out of a country on the brink of anarchy and despair Tito created a power in world politics, a civilised, contented people. He was a wonderful man.

I met him just the once. It was a long day's pony trek to his H.Q. at Jaice. Fitzroy Maclean was there, leading the Allied mission with Randolph Churchill, rather an extrovert character, drinking vodka and throwing out bets that he'd climb the local peak against anyone for a tenner. Still he had the right spirit, easily the eldest of us, asking for no concessions, standing his corner in a parachute drop as well as at the table. He took me in to see the great man, he was the sort you met once or twice in a lifetime, magnetic, Popski was like that; I think Bader must have been. Medium height, fortyish, a dark square man, unsmiling, keen eyes fixed at you. There was an interpreter beside him.

> "You burned the glider!" he said abruptly.
> "Yes Sir! I'm sorry"
> "Why?" he leaned forward.

I had no hesitation in shopping his minions at Petrovac. "It was

the only way I could think of to get them moved", I answered. I gave him an account of the whole thing, but he raised his hand to cut me short and briefly glanced aside before fixing his eyes on me again. "It was a pity, but you did well; give my thanks to your pilots."
I saluted and walked out, but I have never forgotten those few minutes and those blazing eyes.

The days did not drag. I spent quite a deal of time learning Serbo-Croat. Two of the Mission officers had a primer and they practised translating the exercises from English, while I tried to translate back without cribbing the answer. These fellows were of a predictable pattern. Their unit at Bari was known as 133 Force. I gathered there were similar units in plenty in London, Cairo, Algiers, all the same in essentials. The Cloak and Dagger brigades. Liaison with resistance groups everywhere was their job and of course many of them; male and female, were leading hazardous lives and suffering tortured deaths but our lot were not all that impressive. The British were invariably Oxbridge men, from the same public schools, from the same prep. schools even. Not too bright as scholars and less so as soldiers, but I could not help recognising that they had a kind of style, an inability to recognise or acknowledge danger, an enviable free-masonry, a casual sloppy way of approaching difficulties that all too often actually worked. They were like actors underplaying a part. Soldiering was an amateur game as far as officers were concerned; the sergeants were the pros. They pulled my leg quite a bit and behind my back called me the Cock Pheasant. At my school we had never been taught that if you happen to excel at anything it isn't supposed to show.

Just one night I went out into the woods with about ten of the Drugs, a couple of them girls. We called at two or three forest huts. Crossed an open road, timber close on either side, no traffic. It was easier going under the trees where the snow was thinner, but the walking was very exhausting. Sometime in the middle of the night we all rested at a large hut in a ravine where we had a delicious fry-up. Like real bacon. Towards dawn, exhausted and foot-sore in my clumsy flying boots, I was glad when they broke into song the signal that we were nearly home. It was nice. The British Army never sang, not spontaneously on the march as they did in the Great War. It harked back to my childhood, listening in the dark of a Saturday night to the harmony that distance lends to the singing of tipsy men homeward bound.

My billet was very comfortable. A farmhouse on the edge of town, its ground floor was devoted to the cows and two ponies and a store of hay and turnips. A ladder led to the central upstairs landing from which the living and bedrooms led off. The cattle helped to keep it warm and it was scrupulously clean, and no fleas! The head of the house was our landlady, a good-looking sturdy woman of around 50. After we'd been there about five weeks I began to sense that I was overdue for a bath. I wasn't looking forward to it in the freezing conditions, but took my little tin wash bowl for a fill of water, set it down in the middle of the floor and stripped off. I was just pondering on the modus operandi as I could only get one foot at a time in the bowl when up went the wooden hatch and in came the good lady with an armful of bedding. She stopped on the threshold as I grabbed my towel, dropped the bedding, raised her hands with a little "Woopsie" and shot off out again. I'd no sooner closed the door and set my towel aside when in she came again, this time trundling a half-barrel washtub which she spun handily to a standstill beside me. Next journey she struggled in with a three gallon pail of hot water, steaming beautifully. She then emptied my tin bowl into the tub and motioned to me to follow it, and before I could blink, snatched my towel away and set about me. She had a kind of cocoa-matting hand scrubber and I swear she went over me every inch with it. There was no time for embarrassment. It was agony! I was sure I could feel the skin peeling off my back. She had to crouch down while she emptied a bowl of water over my head, then stand up again while she poured more over my shoulders. Only then did she stand back, arms akimbo, to look at her handiwork. Then with a nod and a smile she picked up my towel, flung it at me and went. Bless her! The day we went I gave her my last tablet of soap that I'd been hoarding and she held it lovingly against her cheek and tearfully bobbed her thanks. Within a month the Germans were to re-occupy the town and many's the time over the years I've thought of my brave little landlady and hoped they did her no harm. Her kind, in any country, anytime, are the salt of the earth. Don't talk to me about partisans!

Well, that's about all there is to say about Bunghole. We'd watched the snow shrinking in the lovely March weather.

We'd been the first aircraft in and five weeks later we were in the first aircraft out. Air Commodore Whitney Strought, a famous multi-millionaire Grand Prix racing driver of those days, brought in his C47 and then, after throwing out everything detachable, seats, parachutes, doors, all our kit and arms, he took it off again, bumping desperately over the uneven hillside, still covered with nearly a foot of snow, to lift off at the last second to brush through the tree-tops to turn south for Italy. Two hours later we tumbled out half frozen at Bari.

I still had to face a debriefing at 133 Force, but I thought we'd done pretty well. I got a real snotty-nosed Yes Minister type. I'd lived in my clothes for over a month and was not feeling ready to be looked up and down as if I'd been a bad smell. Well he needn't have made it quite so obvious.
"What have you got to say about that glider? The Drugs are furious because it was theirs after you landed. The Americans are mad because it was theirs before that, and I'm annoyed because I've had to tear up the court-martial papers I'd got out for you."
He quite took the wind out of my sails. All I could think of to say was, "Would that be because the glider had never been theirs anyway?"
"Don't be impertinent" he snapped. "We've torn up your recommendation and you can think yourself lucky!"
I turned my back on him and walked out. Bugger 'em I thought. At any rate, after I'd cooled down I put Sergeants Andy McCulloch and Jock Morrison (the other two pilots) in for

DFMs and they came through a week or two later.

It was a warm spring afternoon as I walked through the olive groves and vines to the farmhouse mess back at Comiso. Robbie Coulthard and Teddy Hain were snoring after their lunch. It transpired there'd been a reported crash over Split the day we'd gone in and somehow I'd got mixed up with this other poor sod and been posted missing a month back. However it was all exaggerated as they say so we opened up the bar and some of the Yanks looked in and the Pathfinders and that was that. Opening my mail I learned that Chris had been born a week before I left, and was already six weeks old, luckily there'd been just enough doubt about that crash for them to hang on for confirmation so there was no harm done at home. But just then, Comiso felt like home and it felt good to be back.

Chapter 7
Invasion of Southern France

Ponte Olivio, Gela, Sicily. A good place to fly from though the little town was a bit of an eyesore, 2500 years ago all this coast from Syracuse west to Agrigento had been part of the empire of Ancient Greece. The poet Aeschylus had gazed on this same high outline of hills to the north marching in on this narrow plain between the mountains and the sea, and surely he had been the first recorded victim of aerial bombardment, killed, they say, by a turtle, dropped on his head by a passing eagle! I was to be presented to General Eaker, Deputy Supreme Commander, Med., who pinned the American silver pilot's wings on my shirt. I couldn't wear them of course - I've got them about somewhere. I dutifully told him that his Col. Duden had made it easy for us, though at the time I'd feared he was going to land us in Romania. On the way back to Comiso the tow-rope snapped and I had to make a shaky landing on the cliff-top; the Waco was not much damaged and was soon flying again, but I got my leg pulled as a Jinx when I got back, for they had already christened me "Crash" from an earlier do at Gela.

This earlier crash had been a real up and downer. We'd been hanging about waiting for a glider to be tested after repair, and to save time I said I would fly it with the Yank Chief Engineer, Archie Moore, and off we went. Archie was in trouble right away, the nose would not come up, the C47 was away above us and we were hanging on its tail. We were 1000ft up and there

THE HORSA GLIDER

was a terrific "slap, slap" behind us, like loose control cables cracking against the canvas roof. We could stall the tow-ship at any second and Archie, pulling back on the stick with all his strength, welled out to "punch the tit", and I let the rope go. The C27 soared away and we just went into a diving parabola, quite out of control, and hit the deck at 100mph.

I was sitting on the field, looking round for the glider. The sun was still there, the grass nice and warm. I must have been unconscious. The width of a football pitch away the 'blood wagon' was parked beside a tangle of metal tubing where they were fishing out poor Archie. There was nothing more to be seen but shattered sheets of plywood and torn canvas flapping in the wind. They looked as if they were scratching about to find the other body so I got up and walked across. They never quite worked out where I'd come from. You never know with crashes.

I saw Archie, in hospital at Palermo; he had a broken back but was cheerful enough to tell anyone who would listen about this Limey guy who'd yelled out "Pick your feet up! Hug your knees! Roll yourself into a ball!" So that was how I came to be called "Crash" which stuck to me throughout the rest of my army career. Archie was invalided Stateside as they used to say, but although a bit sore I hadn't a scratch to show. A year later, when I was going parachuting, the doctor told me I'd broken my arm in the recent past which had healed itself perfectly. It often happens, he said.

The Cockpit of the Horsa Glider.
By kind permission of The Assault Glider Trust, Lichfield.

Around about that time we had started ferrying gliders from Casablanca to Bizerta and thence to Sicily to be later ferried up to the Rome area for the invasion of Southern France. So I was doing quite a bit of flying back and forth along the North African coast, and one day I ran into a young French 2nd Lieutenant at Tunis who was looking for a ride to Algiers. He was very young, obviously in a brand new uniform, and not very sure of himself so I got him on our plane and off we went.

When we landed at Maison Blanche neither of us had a billet to go to. The weather turned bitterly cold and the plane was grounded for a few days for repairs (well, you'd expect that from the Yank aircrews with a chance of a week in Algiers). So we were both grateful for the offer of accommodation at the American Red Cross. It was one of the biggest hotels in the city and I remember there was a half flight of wide stairs leading up to a reception desk on the landing with a couple of French girls checking us into our rooms as we slowly shuffled upwards. Jean was immediately in front of me as he came up to the table.

"Name!" the little French piece bent over her lists.

"Aumont!" replied Jean.

"First name please!" she demanded.

"Jean-Pierre!" said he.

"Jean-Pierre" she repeated to herself as she scribbled away; "Jean-Pierre Aumont". And then after a seconds pause she slowly raised her eyes and sank back with a gasp as the pencil fell from her fingers.

"Jean-Pierre Aumont!" She turned to her companion;

The Inside of The Horsa Cockpit

By kind permission of The Assault Glider Trust, Lichfield.

"C'est Jean-Pierre Aumont!". More screams and gasps and a minor pandemonium as it turned out that my mate of the last couple of days had been the leading heart-throb of the French cinema.

When the excitement had died down we went into the huge lounge full of rowdy untidy Americans with whom Jean cut no ice at all. However one of them edged forward.
>"You can't be the French guy who's married to Maria Montez", he challenged.
>"Yes" said Jean, "Maria is my wife.
>"Say fells," he swung around. "This guy is married to Maria Montez."

And this did cut the ice. Jean may have been an unknown stranger but Maria Montez was quite different. She was a young South American starlet whose outstanding beauty had got her a contract at Hollywood; I'd seen her photo in the film magazines but never in a picture, a film I mean. Her sort of film was more suited to the little hick townships of America. "Daughter of the Thief of Baghdad" was more her style. Still she was obviously nationally known in the States and the motley pilots gazed at Jean in undisguised envy. Strange the way things work out; within a few years the gorgeous Maria was to be found dead in her bath, whilst the unknown Jean-Pierre Aumont became and remains to this day, forty years later, one of the outstanding actors of the French theatre.

Not so many days after the Generals Parade, at Gela, I went up on short attachment to the Para Brigade who were in the front line in Italy. The fighting had got bogged down all this winter about a hundred kilometres Northeast of Naples. There was the wide valley, the Apennines rising on either side thousands of feet above the valley floor where the flood-swollen Garigliano river meandered down from the massive bastion of rock at the head of the valley upon which the Monastery of Monte Cassino looked out over the feeble struggles and the privations of the soldiery beneath its shadow. We lived in shallow trenches a foot deep in water, our heads below ground level all the daylight hours, every inch of ground swept by the enemy machine-gun and artillery fire. Thankfully we were only there a week before being relieved, wretched with hunger, wet and cold, sleepless and grey-faced. The day before, apparently out of patience with the weeks and months of deadlock, the Americans seemed to go mad; in a daylong blasting of the whole of the northern end of the valley they sent over every bomber they could get into the air. It was frightful. There was nothing to be seen of Monte Cassino until the smoke and dust had cleared away the following day. Bombs fell everywhere, often miles from their target as if thrown out haphazard by giants' hands. The air thudded against the eardrums, the ground heaving like an earthquake. It was a slaughter, a savage pumping of death, without reply, into the enemy position as it was thought to be. A week later the 8th Army, in the shape of some Poles and New Zealanders I think, stormed the desecrated height and broke through; and within a day the month's long battle was over.

It was a month later that Bill Needle asked me if I'd like to go up with him on a Good-time-Charlie trip up to Anzio where the Yanks had at last broken clear of the beaches towards the outskirts of Rome. My cousin Mary reminded me years later that I had written to her about that time. How we struggled zigzagging along the valley between the bomb craters, stopping to cool down beneath the unrecognisable face of the Monastery. The whole earth was churned up like a Christmas pudding in the making. Rough crosses had fallen askew in the liquid mud and here and there a rusty rifle topped by a steel helmet stuck out of the tortured earth, and over all the smell of death still hung like a blanket. This is how it was to die in battle as Britons, Americans, Germans and Italians, Poles, New Zealanders and Gurkhas had died here. Regardless of country, to my mind that day, you couldn't but salute them; - all men who fought here had done well.

We went on towards Rome, and the following day were borne on the tide of American troops struggling into the celestial city, beneath the walls of the Coliseum, within sight of the dome of St. Peters itself, the hysterical people milling and crushing around us, I recalled how back in England on the cinema news I had enviously watched Monty's lot, marching into Tripoli, the Desert Rats, every man an emperor and wondering if I might be there when we marched into Rome. And there we were, the cheers, the girls, the wine, everything, never to be forgotten.

At the end of April we left Sicily for the last time. We were moving up into Italy to an airfield at Gaudo about ten kilometres south of Salerno. This is a very pleasant country at this time of the year though all around Salerno was evidence of bitter fighting the previous autumn when the 8th Army had been moving up towards Naples. The 64th Troop Carrier Wing was still with us, and, having seen all the gliders away I left Comiso as passenger in a C47. Flying north from Catania that day I must have flown almost directly over my very first landing on Sicily nearly a year before. Etna was turning out a thick plume of vapour; then, Sicily left behind, the fireworks display of Stromboli rose out of the sea dead ahead. Two hours more and we had flown past Salerno and over the ruins of Pompeii so that the pilot could give us a close-up view of Vesuvius in full eruption belching fire and brimstone into the heavens, the smoke of its craters blackening the sky as far as the eye could see, its dust settling inches deep as much as twenty miles away, a black rain of pumice dust. So we saw Europe's three volcanoes all in eruption on the same day; it must have been a unique sight.

At Gaudo we were still following in the footprints of the Greeks of old, for right here in the edge of the airfield stood the great sandy-grey pile of the Temple of Neptune, one of the wonders of the ancient world. The old Italian curator showed us on a model how it had been built. Take a good site with rock available and to that you add a thousand slaves. Lay down your first course moving the massive stones on timber rollers into their appointed places. Then bury the whole layer flush with the ground, then bung up your next course and bury it again, and so continue until all you can see is a little mountain of earth, topped by the last course of the roof coping. Then you dig it all out and your temple really is unveiled for the very first time. Stonehenge must have been built the same way thousands of years before. This was the Greek province of Paestum, one of the outposts of their Italian empire.

Jutting out into the sea to the north was the scenic Amalfi peninsular with the island of Capri lying off its tip. The Germans had sensibly used Amalfi and Sorrento as delectable leave camps for their Africa Corps but the whole area had been so smashed up in the fighting as to be impassable even to Jeeps and the road from Salerno, 50 kms, to Naples, by-passed it, crossing the base of the peninsular through Castelamare, where we came on to the very first motorway we had ever seen, dead straight to Naples. It should have been straight but it was a tortuous progress through the bomb and demolition craters, and my first sight of Naples was a miserable one indeed, the pouring rain bringing down the volcanic cloud overhead, every vehicle and building streaked with the never ending rain of black sludge. But when the rain stopped and the sun came through it brought out the girls on the Via Roma like crocuses in spring. But they could not hide the ugliness of this cesspool of a city. You can live with poverty in the hills and out in the country but in Naples it had an ugliness and a stink that was sickening.

Only a day or two later came the news-flash of the long-awaited Second Front; the invasion of Northern France had begun. We in the Med. were already familiar with the expression D-day. We had had plenty already from Alamein to

Casablanca, Tobruk to Taranti, Syracuse to Anzio. But now for the first time the press and radio had a headline they could print large; it was the one they had all been waiting for.

We had already guessed that our own next D-day could not be far away. All this time we had continued the steady stream of gliders up from the African ports, Horsas and Wacos, packing them in where we could like cars in a car park. The Paras and Gliders had done well in Normandy but there had been lessons to learn and we set to work to show what the veterans could do. In takeoff practice we'd been getting the trains into the air, one every two minutes, then we halved the time and puzzled and experimented to halve it again. By August we had three trains rolling down the runway at one time, 30 seconds apart, with the Yanks competing with us, stopwatches and all, a new record everyday. By now we had moved up once more from Salerno to an airfield 10 kms north of Rome called Marcigliano and by the first week in August we knew we were bound for the South of France, the Cote d'Azure, Monte Carlo and all that. Our exact target was a road, rail and river bridge junction ten minutes flight inland from Cannes, at a little town called Le Muy.

Our squadron was to head the operation, flying 36 Horsa gliders, to be followed by 450 American Wacos. Over 200 Jeeps, 200 guns, bulldozers and scrapers for airfield construction, explosives, ammunition, rations. They asked us how much landing space we needed and we happened on a tattered copy of Picture Post with an aerial photo of the most crowded area of the Normandy landings they could find. Scaled up we counted 30 gliders in an area around 300 yards square. On the premise that what's been done before can be done again better, we asked for an area 250 yards square for our 36. The 1st Independent Glider Squadron, to give its army description, commanded by Major Robbie Coulthard, was divided into three flights led by me (also acting second in command), Johnnie Mockridge, and Wally Masson. In addition I had a flight second Teddy Hain. Robbie was to head the whole Armada, No1 in an echelon of 9. Thirty seconds behind I came with the 2nd echelon numbers 10 to 18. Then John with 19 to 27 and Wally with 28 to 36. That was the theory. You have to have a landing plan even though you know that in the event, for a hundred obvious reasons, it will not work. After all the first one to land has a nice area to himself, while No.29 will in theory find 19 gliders scattered all over the place in front of him. Not only that but if you stray outside your target you are getting under the wheels of the other four hundred, desperately looking for a place to put down. *"The accompanying sketches show how we took off and how we hoped to land.* TakeOff: *No 1 tow ship pulls out (there's a spare tow rope alongside the runway to show the exact tightening point) takes the strain and moves No. 1 glider off. The instant it is clear (and he's already been inching forward against his brales) out comes No. 2 tow ship. He's got his glider moving as No.1 is halfway down the runway. Then No. 3 moves out as No. 1 takes off at the far end of the runway. Simple enough; but it takes practice when the air is full of the thunder of seventy engines. Clouds of dust cover everything*

GLIDER TAKE OFF PLAN

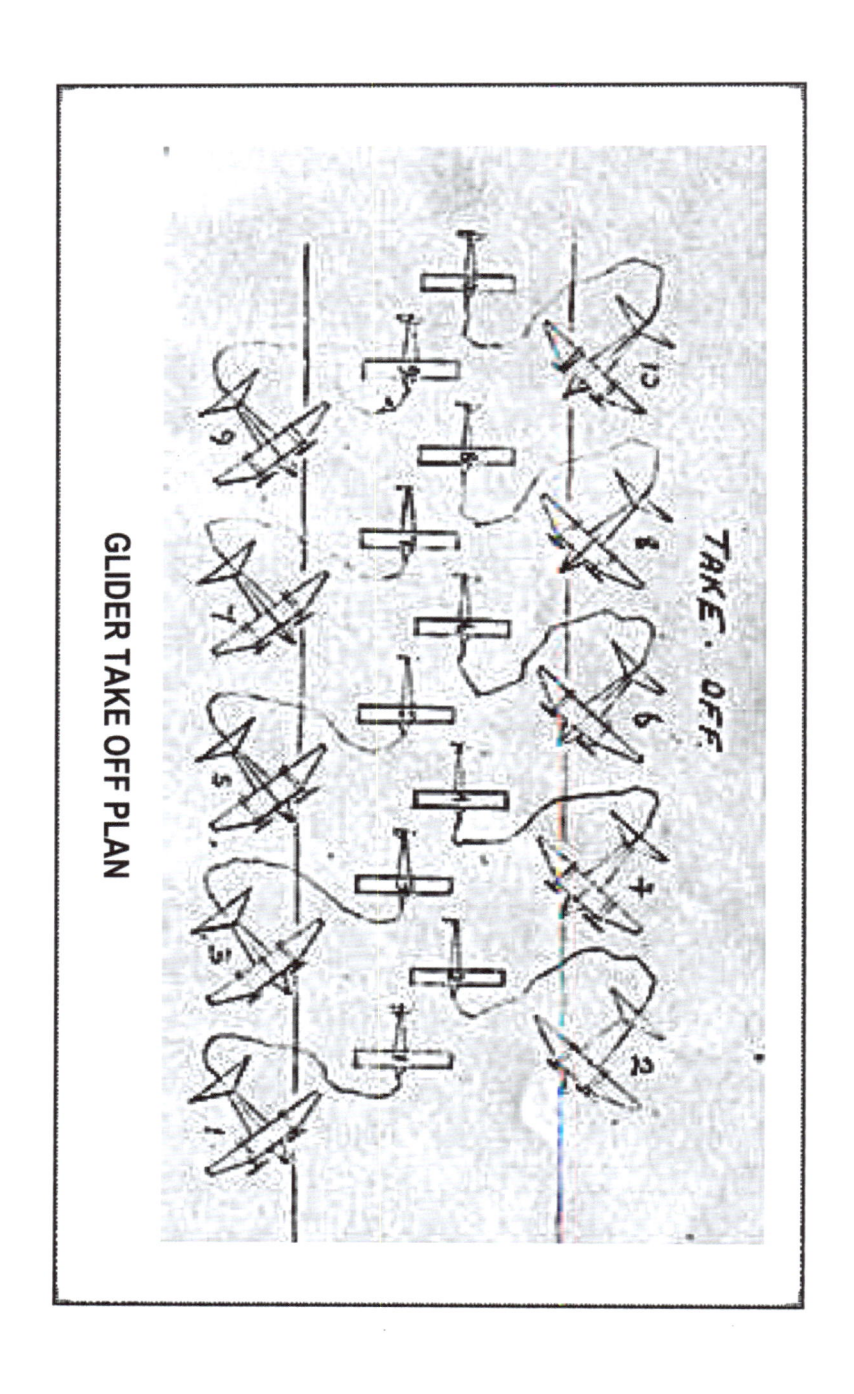

like a thick fog and tow ropes writhe like deadly snakes along the ground. Landing: *This is what it is meant to look like provided we actually got there, all of us. Remember we expected wings to be torn off crashing into trees and other gliders, undercarriages to collapse; gliders to catch fire, turn over, cartwheel – and so they did!* "

The photos showed our area to be covered with small trees and we hoped they were young fruit trees which would not seriously affect the Horsas. We went over the plan, the maps, and the photos until we dreamt about them. I still do. And then 14th August came the word. It's on! D-day tomorrow! Take-off 05.30. Landfall Cannes 07.30, 15th August 1944.

So far as we were concerned Operation Dragoon went off as near perfection as you are ever likely to get in a turn-out of this size. We were off to the second, having been up most of the night. We'd been in the air well over an hour when the leading tow-ships suddenly banked round and the whole shebang headed back to Italy and by 08.00 we were landing back at our starting point at Tarquinia. There was a rumour that the Navy had scrubbed the whole thing, that they'd got nervous as they had got Churchill on a battleship somewhere, watching the affair like a football match. What a let down! But wait, here comes the Base Commander. How long would it take to set up the gliders again? - You tell us. Two hours? Yes, we'd be ready in two hours. And then the pandemonium. Re-testing of engines and release gear. Gliders being dragged back from every corner of the airfield. Controls to check, ropes to snake out, maps to check. By mid afternoon we were airborne once

THE GILDER LANDING PLAN!

more, steering fair for France, course 300 in a cloudless sky! Elba down there under the starboard wing, the northern tip of Corsica dim in the distance ahead.

This time it went like a dream. There was the coast, no imagination this time: white buildings, red cliffs, timber. There was the island Santa Margherita and the glaring white front of Cannes with the timbered hills behind. Ships? we'd never heard of rocket ships; much less seen them, spouting their hundreds of streaking missiles ahead of us. Then we were over the land, ten minutes to go. I'd already drawn the track on my, map, divided into ten one minute sections. One minute, two minutes, three minutes, all forest and rocky hills below - tracer like toy fireworks lazily curving up and away. On my wing the other gliders gently rocking steadily along. Sergeant Harry Lansdell keeps his eyes rock-steady ahead staring along the tow-trope. Four minutes. Over my shoulder, over the bonnet of the jeep the eyes of the Gunnery Sgt. Major stared past me as I gave him a grin and a thumbs up. Five minutes. Lots of smoke below, the forest well alight but we are on track. Good old Peter Baker - his pathfinders are guiding us bang on. Six minutes - Whoops! that was a near one and the Horsa lurched for a moment but Harry gave no sign, his knuckles white on the control column. Seven, the craggy hills dead ahead and to port the flat cultivation in the river valley. Eight minutes and there was the town, Le Muy; there was the railway and on towards the north the river gorge. We were going to do it. Nine minutes, there's the L.Z. a square field, one corner cut off, the country road beyond. Time for Robbie dead ahead to let his rope go - there, well done Robbie. Their tow-ships flying straight on, Robbie followed by his other eight gliders swing round to the left. My hand reached down for the rope release lever, a firm tug and away goes the rope. Now gently, all we have to do is put this old lady down there.

"Dead ahead, you've got 1000 feet, 80 knots, 90 degrees to port" Harry dipped the port wing as we came across track and there for the first time I saw the sky behind us, dark with a thousand aircraft, close packed as far as the eye could see. "Seven hundred feet, 75 knots, bring her round again 90 degrees. Right. I've got her!" As I took the wheel Harry leaned back and took up the instrument readings without a break. "Five hundred, 70 knots, four hundred"; now round for the landing. Robbie's glider disappeared into the boundary hedge in a cloud of dust. "Twenty seconds Sergeant major - hold tight" I called over my shoulder. We were hitting anti-landing poles as big as telegraph poles, knocking them down like dominoes as we came to a stop. I breathed out. "Well done Harry!"

The gunners were out already, fanned out and among the vines, like on an exercise. I pulled the lever that should have blown the tail off with an explosive charge. Nothing! So they set to work to hack it off with axes. I climbed on to the roof and looked about. John Mockridge called across from thirty yards away; "OK Crash?" As I waved back I watched Wally settle beside him gentle as a feather. And suddenly the air was full of Wacos landing in all directions at all speeds, crashing, stalling, cart-wheeling. We kept our heads down for ten minutes and then it was over. By now our gunners had got their jeeps and guns away and the Yanks were picking themselves out of the wreckage, lighting cigars and shambling off down the road in the general direction of the war.

It took some time to cut Robbie out of his glider. He had two broken legs and as it turned out the war for him was over. Teddy Hain, our operatic tenor finished his war here as well; he'd finished up upside down with a jeep on top of him and was lucky to get way with a broken back. Sergeant Jenner had been hit in the air, point blank, as he was landing and was killed as he crashed straight into the German gun-post, wiping it out. Half of us had already flown over it at tree top height. This was the one and only time in the whole war that I got within stones throw of the opposition, and within an hour all the Germans within a mile of us were behind barbed wire.

Finding myself for the first time in command of the squadron, I joined up with Peter Baker's Pathfinders and we made ourselves useful cutting out and clearing a light aircraft landing strip and collecting and organising the hundreds of containers that came down by parachute. That first night, our first in France, we turned in like the birds at dusk, tired out as much by the sheer excitement of it all as by our labours since reveille at 4 a.m. at Tarquinia, we purloined some wine from a nearby barn where the casks had come under fire; then we rigged parachutes overhead to keep off the dew, and piled them up in dozens to make a bed of unimagined luxury and slept like the dead. Hardships? I tell you!

We had a conference later giving orders to move back to the coast where we made camp in a lovely pine grove on the cliffs above Cap d'Antibes. In to Cannes the next day for new orders to expect embarkation any day back to Rome. Hanging about in the heat of the afternoon I dropped into a large cafe, its walls lined by mirrors, fronting the town square. I ordered a glass of wine and the waiter was anxious to show off his English. He nodded towards the square; "They bring out girls who sleep with German soldiers." Farm wagons were drawing up across the head of the square, forming a platform that was filling up with drab little men, members of the Resistance my waiter said, the so-called Marquis, the first time I'd seen them. Someone made a short speech and there was flag waving, hammer and sickle, Cross of Lorraine, cheers and raucous cackling laughter. Then, suddenly a screaming girl was dragged forward, stripped to the waist, and thrown into a chair and held there spread eagled, a man on each arm, as the speech continued with whistles, jeers, screams and howls from the mob below. As he finished a huge slatternly woman stepped up to the struggling girl, seized her by the hair and with a pair of sheep-shears began to carve it off in great handfuls. Within a few seconds she was roughly shorn to the scalp, and thrown down to the crowd as a second victim was dragged forward. Was this what we were fighting for? I looked away, feeling sick, and there in one of the mirrors covering the cafe walls and pillars I saw a girl's face. A young, pretty face whose eyes were wide with horror, obviously fixed in terror on the scene outside. I didn't look round for the owner of the face. Those trembling parted lips could have screamed out beyond control if our eyes had met. Head down I pushed back my chair and hurried out and away. Not for the first time I had a glimpse of the unacceptable face of freedom. Overnight it seemed France was free, De Gaulle parading down the Champs Elysees, and the lights on again at the Moulin Rouge. But my business was soldiering and within a week we were scrambling up nets in the middle of the night to board a ship at Frejus bound for Italy.

Chapter 8
Italy, Greece and the End of the War

Back at Tarquinia a new Commanding Officer, Major McMillan had arrived directly from England and I reverted to my position of second in command. I had been made up to captain and with increased strength with the draught of pilots 'Mac' had brought out with him, John Mockridge and Wally Masson got their three pips as well. I now found myself glider spokesman in the planning of future operations. This did not weigh heavily. My general approach was to say "Yes" to everything. Unknown to us the great airborne operation to Arnhem was ready to go. A landing in the Po valley would have to be put off until the spring if only because we should not be able to get enough gliders available for another landing like the South of France. On the other hand Churchill had always had a soft spot for Greece. Though the whole of Greece and the Balkans were still in German occupation five years to the day since the outbreak of war, someone decided that they were ripe for liberation, a nice little job for the 2nd parachute Brigade and the 1st Independent Glider Squadron.

Scattered around the Rome area were about two hundred Wacos rejected by the Yanks who had followed us into "Dragoon" and we had to get enough of these together to go into Greece. John Mockridge got plenty to help from our old side-kicks the 64th T.C. engineers and in a week they'd earmarked a bunch of the least forlorn looking; with some hiccups we managed to fly them down to Manduria in the heel

The 1st Independent Squadron GPR in front of a Horsa Glider.
Corney standing on extreme left.

of Italy, not far from Brindisi. All sorts of pieces had fallen off on the way down but we got about 40 there somehow. McMillan, judging them on the standards current back home, was appalled I'm afraid we pulled his leg with our blasé attitude of "well we've always got there so far".

The Pathfinders were as usual to lead in on D-1; a third of the Paras and six gliders with special loads would go on D-day, followed by the rest of the Brigade and Gliders, with container drops to follow as needed. L.Z. was a dirt strip at Megara, a little coastal town halfway between Corinth and Athens. Yes, in all the apparent chaos of last minute preparations, the ancient names gave us a thrill. D-day was eventually fixed for Friday 13th October. The Pathfinders had already got away in the night and we'd heard that they were on the target. I was on the runway early with Harry Landsell marshalling the first glider flight for take-off, with Major McMillen at the head. At this moment up drove the Brigade second-in-command. Now Col. Alistair Pearson was one more of those fire-eating men who'd led a charmed life; he had already won two D.S.O.'s and was no man to argue with. What was McMillen thinking about, flying off and leaving his squadron behind. "We don't work that way in the 2nd Para Brigade" he thundered, "Where's Turner?" I was in my runway outfit, just shorts and gym-shoes flagging forward the first C47. "Get out McMillen, get in Turner. Got a map?˙ Know where to go? OK Wave them off McMillen!" Harry Landsell just had time to scramble in beside me and we were on our way, rising into a fine still morning sky, eastward bound.

As usual I left the flying to Harry as I sorted through someone else's maps and looked round the glider to see what we'd got. It all looked neatly stored, secured and labelled. Just wooden crates; 4000 lbs of high explosives and demolition stores. Well, I was not going to lose any sleep over it now, but it would have been more comfortable for one and all if they had been marked "Senior Service" or "Johnny Walker"! We left the Albanian coast and Corfu on the port quarter and an hour after take-off were approaching Patras at the western end of the Gulf of Corinth. Must be a good tail wind. Good Waco too. Harry as ever was firm and steady as the Sphinx. Friday 13th, 4000 lbs of high explosive, ah well. Whoever was in the C47 ahead of us, he was dead on track. We came up towards the Canal; a clean sliced wedge cut through the isthmus, it looked hundreds of feet deep, a proper engineering job. A burst of tracer cut short our admiration, curving up and away behind us. Not a bad position to be, No.1, you get a good view. Ten minutes from the Canal to Megara, lower hills now to port, the sea to starboard. A white town half a mile inland left and a high headland right with a large island beyond, pale grey on an inky sea. Salamis; we were there! The strip between the town and the sea. More ack-ack! No, it's Peter's verey-light signal, and his smoke - what a wind - from the north too - we'd have to go half way round again. I hit the button and let the rope go, bringing Harry round left on to our reciprocal, over the town, left again out over the foreshore and the sea 400 feet and the last 90° turn to come over the headland. Down, down, perfect Harry, 100 feet, over the strip and touch-down, gentle as a gull.

"Well done Harry, sorry I forgot to take over!"

And there was Peter and Dumbo Willans and Jock Boyd, all smiles "Nice trip?" "Not bad. How's the local talent?" "Well - you know."

There was no time for back-slapping. A Jerry detachment was dug in at a culvert half a mile away and Peter was keeping their heads down with the help of a score of Partisans. He had half a dozen plane loads of the 4th Battalion coming in an hour behind us, and left me and my lads with Dumbo to look after the verey-lights for the drop while he went after the Jerries. It was blowing a full gale by the time the C47s came in with the drop and the thing was a bit of a disaster. Many of the Paras who hadn't been able to get out of their harness (as the old hands did) were swept off the D.Z. like autumn leaves and dragged over the foreshore rocks and bashed to pieces. They lost a round dozen dead, including Lieut. Marsh who had won the Sword of Honour at Sandhurst only months before. Next day the wind had dropped, and the rest of the Brigade and McMillen with our gliders came in more or less without further calamity. There were parachutes everywhere and soon the women began coming nervously down from the town begging for them; with no clothing materials for years but rough home-spun wool, the 'chutes must have looked to them like manna from heaven.

I'd found some uniform stores among the canisters and put on a pair of battledress trousers to supplement my scanty rig-out.

We were gathering the canisters into some sort of order when I suddenly felt an agonising knife-stab pain right on my tail! Staff-Sergeant Tom Gillies was just beside me. "For God's sake come and look what I've got in my pants," I yelled, diving for the door of the nearest glider, dropping my pants on the way. "Look out," someone shouted "It's a scorpion!" But no help to me. They had me spread-eagled on my tummy and trouserless, opened a Red Cross canister and dressed my swiftly swelling bum with iodine from a tube like toothpaste, while the ladies joined the gathering crowd offering, no doubt, the best Greek advice. My groans were genuine but lost on the sergeants who fell about laughing. For days afterwards as I limped about the town I could see the black-clad matrons and giggling girls nudging each other and grinning behind their hands as they sat, endlessly tatting, beside the doors of their white shining cottages.

Within a couple of days the Germans were clear of Athens and on their way north, so the Partisans judged it safe to come down from the hills, bearded desperadoes, bandoleers criss-crossed over their chests. Quite impressive they were at first sight, picturesque certainly, as they welcomed us grandly, offering the freedom of their country with open arms and bottles of wine, but by now we were not without experience and it was not long before we had their measure for what partisans too often were, a bunch of loud-mouthed layabouts with an eye on the main chance, who had spent their time Jerry-dodging in the hills, and were now in town for pickings. They soon grew sullen when we made it clear that it was we who were taking over the town, that we had no time for them or their racketeering, so, with dark threats they followed the Brigade into Athens and we were left to garrison the town.

Megara was a substantial country town of around 5000 people, midway between Corinth and Athens, set back the part of a mile from the seashore, on the lower foothills of an amphitheatre of mountains to the north, rising to perhaps for businessmen from the capital 25 miles to the east, more recently occupied by Germans. But the bulk of the population lived in single storey primitive whitewashed cottages. You wouldn't say working population because practically no-one was at work. There was no work and no way of paying wages. You had only to bend your back to pick out of the gutter brand new notes of 10,000 million drachma. There was no coal or other fuel, no trains, no public transport, no power, no lighting. potatoes, maize, olives and grapes had been harvested, the harvesters paid in kind. There was practically no meat or milk. But one thing they had, just one advantage, they had been here before, they'd seen it all, they and their fathers. Saracens, Turks, Bulgars and Germans had followed the Trojans of ancient days, a new tide every generation it seemed, and when the invaders wearied, they'd enough spirit to find good reasons to fight among themselves. They had that spirit and it had been their salvation. There's a lot of rot talked about and written about national spirit in times of war. We stand too close to see ourselves in perspective. But, make no mistake, for all their failings, they have a national character wrought and tempered over the centuries; the best of the Greeks are among the best in the world.

A few days after our arrival at Megara, Major McMillen was invalided home and once more I took over the Squadron. He'd only been with us six weeks and never seemed to have entered into our particular style of soldiery. Every one of the sergeants was known to John, Wally and me by his first name or nickname as a matter of course, but it didn't do for Mac. Then I got the power station manager, the Schoolmaster, and a marvellous giant of a man called George Trippos, the chief miller, and with Wally and John we went over the town, the mills and the power station. There was no language difficulty as most of the older generation of the men had spent years in the States, or on the High Seas. The power man said all his generators needed was diesel, they might go on petrol but he wasn't sure they wouldn't blow up. We'd a couple of sergeants who'd worked in electricity, Leadbetter and Newman. Droop Newman had been my second dickie on "Bunghole" and owed his nickname to an affectation of casual sloppiness put on to get himself noticed. He was one of the best. He and Leadbetter would take charge of the electricity supply, get the town wiring repaired and generally put the fear of God into the power station staff. I handed Newman 100 gallons of our transport petrol and left him to get on with it. I had no occasion to speak to him again before he swallowed the anchor and began a new career as miller of his native town as his father had been. He undertook to get all the millers to do the milling for ten percent of the take if we would supply the power. John and the Schoolmaster became Town Mayor and deputy: Wally was town

Quartermaster, food, wine and women coming under his scrutiny, among other duties. Within ten days the town was lit up, the mills rolling, and Wally in the sick-bay!

The Greek Primate, Archbishop Damaskinos became head of the government in Athens, and came out to hold a thanksgiving in our massive church, and Wally and I were much embarrassed to be shoved forward to stand before the golden altar with the venerable hands laid in blessing on our bowed heads. The partisans, now called Elas were making as much trouble as they dared, shooting up the town as soon as it got dark. They were a spineless bunch and kept their heads down in daylight. Not so in Athens. Bitter fighting had broken out there and the Paras were hard-pressed to keep a foothold in the City. Jock Boyd, the pathfinder ex-Glasgow butcher was killed in Constitution Square. He'd been a great friend to us, one of the most experienced Paras, a veteran of the very first airborne operation across the Channel at Bruneval. It was more quiet with us, most of the time. One extra noisy night, Wally lost his cool being unable to sleep and woke me up to go down with him in a borrowed armoured car at two in the morning to shake up the Elas' H.Q. There he stormed into the building while I traversed the gun to point through the front window. When I got in there Wally was standing over the cringing Elas chief, telling him that if the noise did not stop we'd blow his castle apart, drawing the curtains apart to show him the gun muzzle six feet from his nose. The exercise must have done Wally some good for as soon as we got our heads down again he was fast asleep without any noticeable let up in the fire-cracking around us.

When you are in these occupied countries liberation situations, you have to expect every now and then the most Gilbertian situations, what we called monumental cock-ups, your actual Fred Karno syndrome, as an earlier generation might have named it. Such a one blew up now. The Greek National government had decided on a recruiting drive among the populace to form a brand new national Home Guard to see off the Elas, and shoo them, so to say, back into the sewers, and so it was that one day 100 new rifles arrived to await, in our safekeeping, the needs of this local force, the Megara Company of the National Guard. The day of the arrival of the recruiting deputation from Athens was one of our red letter days. We'd heard they were in town but they had not called on us so that afternoon we had a rather heavy poker school going at the Armoured Car lads' Mess down at the power station. Around two o'clock our Staff Sergeant Barker, on orderly duty, interrupted the game to say that the Elas were about to hang the half dozen officers of the deputation. Well, not to worry, they were just sounding off as usual so on with the game. He was soon back with the late bulletin that Elas had got them lined up in the town square, under a cherry tree a-piece with ropes round their necks! So I judged it time to show a little interest.

Wally marched off with that grin on his face to get the flying picket of half a dozen of our lads with an armed jeep; this was right up Wally's alley. John lumbered off to get the rest of the squadron out of the sack, and the Armoured Car Officers strolled off to give their motors a run. I strode down towards the square through the unusual quiet of the town. Half the size of a football pitch, the tree-lined, dirt-floored square was overlooked by the municipal offices across one end as the National Gallery overlooks Trafalgar Square. I came in from the back to find it packed with people, half the town I guessed, with the Elas' hammer and sickle fluttering over all. The wretched recruiting deputation was lined up, tied hand and foot beneath the trees, dangling nooses swinging from the branches overhead, whilst above them some new demagogue I hadn't seen before was doing his blood pressure a mischief yelling and sweeping his arms about. He had me spotted as I made my lonely way through the crowd, parting before me with a low hum that had my spine tingling. Time for the Cavalry I felt, and right on cue into the square behind me roared our Jeep making a fine entry in a cloud of dust. Wally jumped down beside me:

"I've told them to aim high" he said. "They know the drill. Come on. At the crowd rapid fire!" he urged out of the corner of his mouth.

"Really?" I asked.

"Well, look at 'em. What else?"

"Right!" I spun round, took a deep breath so that my voice did not break and yelled in my best barrack square style:

"At the crowd - Rapid - Fire!"

The two machine guns on the Jeep nearly blew my head off as half a dozen quick bursts rang over the crowd as all the windows of the municipal offices disappeared. Just a silence of a second or two before the crowd broke in panic for every exit, screams of women getting trampled, yells of imaginary orders from Wally, another burst, more rushing for the exits and the streets beyond. Pandemonium! From the bonnet of the Jeep I watched the mob fall away from us like straw in the wind. It was the one and only time I ever really saw Wally in his element. "Here!" he shouted, throwing me a rifle, "Take that side and I'll take this. Give 'em the butt end, any you can reach!" and off we strode down the main street from door to door, threatening all and sundry. When we came to a stop a hundred yards on and turned back, the street was empty. Black heads against white walls peeping out of doors and windows, ready to dodge out of sight on the instant. We walked sternly back to the square, fighting to keep our faces straight at the covert grins of the bolder spirits that followed us.

Meanwhile the armoured cars had turned up. Of Elas there was no sign. Sgt. Maj. Cawood was supervising the untying of the bonds of the captive deputation. When we got them down to our H.Q. it appeared that before the balloon went up they had managed to get around a score of recruits, and to these I now issued the rifles as ordered. They were still terror-stricken, looking fearfully over their shoulders, as they handled the rifles as if they were red hot. It was no good. We took the rifles back again to their obvious relief and sent them home. We put the rifles in our armoury and the deputation on a truck for Athens.

So I reported to the Brigadier that so far from arming the Megara Company, I had felt obliged to disarm them and send them home. He was not amused but I felt bound to tell him that we wouldn't have lasted a week in Megara if the Elas had got those rifles, and that we were better off on our own than playing nanny to a useless home guard.

In spite of this incident we continued to get on very well with the townsfolk. Our mess was a pleasant villa on Main Street, with no sort of guard, day or night, and we kept open house whenever possible to listen to their problems. One morning I got and invitation to a christening. Well it wasn't quite my cup of tea, but they were very pressing about it, and would be honoured if we would allow them to show their appreciation of all we had done. It was to be a grand occasion for this was a first born grandson. The grandparents were preparing a great celebration - after all they were very well off; a dozen assorted pigs, sheep and goats, several hectares of maize-land, six or eight olive trees, they were rich indeed.

So I joined the file of townsfolk up the winding hillside path along with our neighbour Tom Trippos who had made his pile in the coal seams of Pennsylvania in the Twenties. His brother George was helping with the wine, his daughter leading the dancers in the courtyard. And with the dancers whirling round with linked handkerchiefs in a wild Cretan jig, all was merry as a marriage ball. Order was commanded as our host made his speech of welcome and glasses were charged for the toast of the day. We drank to the boy, and Tom at my elbow translated it for me, and I looked again at the young couple, radiant in their pride and happiness and raised my glass and drank again repeating the toast through the catch in my throat: "May he live!" I said.

By the end of November Brigadier Pritchard was up to the neck in troubles of his own in Athens where the Brigade was hanging on by its eye-brows with over a hundred casualties already and the Elas threatening to overrun the City. Meanwhile John and the little crew of RAF fitters had been working away on the gliders for I'd said we would have a shot at flying them out again if possible. We knew they would all be needed as there was bound to be some big operation on the Po valley come the spring. The situation was changing hourly in Athens and suddenly the Brigade was getting on top again with the help of reinforcements landing daily at Piraeus. A relief force arrived at Megara and within 48 hours we said goodbye to our friends there, called up our old tow-ships the 64th T.C., and lined up the Wacos to await them at dawn 4th December. Throughout the autumn we had enjoyed lovely weather and this day was no change. It was only a short runway but the Wacos were empty and everyone got off without incident. Harry Lansdell and I led off, circling the strip until all were away but the half dozen wrecks we couldn't repair, then we were away.

It turned out to be one of the worst glider flights I ever made. We had left behind a delectable autumn on the Aegean shores, but this was the first day of winter. We did not see the Gulf of Corinth, our pilot taking a more northerly route over the Greek mountains. Great masses of black clouds towered above us on all sides and we were thrown all over the sky by the turbulence, the tow line in front disappearing into blank nothingness for minutes on end as the C47 battled through the overcast with mountain peaks, black and dreary, only a few hundred feet below us. We had no maps showing this course so it was a great relief to see islands ahead on a grey sea, when it seemed we should be over Italy by now. Both Harry and I were flying in ten minute stretches, pouring with sweat. From setting course at Megara we saw no other glider and seemed lost in a world of our own. It was calmer over the sea and after over three hours on tow, the Italian coast was in sight - we were half way there! By now we had almost lost interest in the ground below, the flight having become a matter of sheer hanging on, but we thought we recognised the fertile irrigated plain of Foggia, then mountains again, snow-capped now. Somewhere down there would be Monte Cassino - memories of last winter. We never saw Rome. Suddenly our C47 dipped his wings and swung round and we let the rope go after nearly seven hours on tow, first roasted then frozen; as we slithered to a standstill we stepped out at Tarquinia exhausted. 'Anyone else arrived?' we asked. 'No.' Well I told the ground crew they would be wasting their time hanging on for the rest, and I staggered off to the Ops tent to sit at the end of the phone and wait.. As a matter of fact five or six did come in in the next hour, and over the next week all but three came home. Two other crews crashed in the Italian mountains and one crew on an island off Albania where the Navy sent in a frigate to rescue them. Every man arrived in some shape eventually and we settled down into winter quarters once more.

We found a new C.O. awaiting us, so once more I reverted to 2nd I/C. Major Stanley Cairns, a Nottingham man, had been with me in Tunis and Taranto. I had lost sight of him when the main body had gone home in November '43 but he had recently been in the Arnhem lot. A quiet, retiring chap who took his work very seriously, he had no inclination for the free and easy association John, Wally and I had developed with the squadron. He'd brought out with him about fifty second pilots with no real gliding experience, none of the self confidence that two years of knocking about the Med had given our lads. They stood in awe of our hardened campaigners and even saluted their officers all the time! Stanley, by the way, had one notable mark on his log-book that had, early on, distinguished him from his colleagues; at flying training school, after a heavy landing in a Tiger Moth, he had got out and bent down to examine the undercarriage and stopped the propeller with his head! - and walked away without a scratch! Not surprisingly, he was everywhere known as "Bullet-nut".

It was getting cool for our tented camp at Tarquinia so we moved down to Lido di Roma into the ruins of what had once been an impressive array of sea-front holiday hotels. It was a miserable place and we were snowed in, without any heating, so John and I set off one day to look over the countryside. Ten kilometres east of Rome on the road to Tivoli we found an empty spa hotel, but the smell was more than we could stomach. Right opposite was the ornamental entrance to what looked like a pretty little castle topping a knoll terraced with vines. Worth a shufti! So, up the hill we went. It wasn't really a castle in spite of the name grandly carved over the main entrance - *Castle Arcione*. Just a country house, quite modern, but with its outer walls and turrets castellated to look like a miniature fortress. The home of a man not too sure of his neighbours. An ancient custodian crept out of the separate service wing and seemed to welcome our interest. On the first floor were the main living rooms with large windows facing on to an inner courtyard and six or seven fine panelled rooms, above that the bedrooms were massively furnished with two and four poster beds and two wonderful bathrooms, one wholly tiled in green and the other in black glass. And where was the *padrione*? Apparently he had recently departed. "Facisti! Caput!" The caretaker drew a finger across his throat and spat good riddance, a terrible grin cracking his toothless visage. In two days we were installed in the lap of luxury. Major Stanley was a bit dazed about it all. "What about the owner?" "Would it be all right?" "What would brigade say?" We soothed him down, begging him to get his head down and his feet up and bother about tomorrow when it came. The brigade was still in Athens anyway and God helps those who help themselves.

Between ourselves we had to admit it was a marvellous piece of luck, the best billet we ever had. The brigadier was obviously green with envy when he did turn up (to show us his brand new D.S.O. we reckoned), but the lads gave him a real smart turn-out and we gave him a real smart turnout and we gave him a real good drink and had him off the premises in no time with congratulations all round.

So began 1945 in pretty good order with the squadron none the less at a loose end. I'd put in a report that we in the Gliders should take a share in the Pathfinder business with, say, a small detachment to be seconded to Peter Blake, to jump with his party ahead of the gliders and home them in on a radio beacon. Brigade agreed so up on the notice board went a request for officers and four sergeants to volunteer for parachute training. By the weekend we'd six sergeants and no officers. "What did I tell you?" said Wally over my shoulder as I read the list, "you might have known these young rookies wouldn't have it - too near the end of the war - here, hand me your pencil". He added his name and mine, and so the two old sweats of the squadron found themselves, early in March, on our way to the Parachute Training School at Gioya del Col between Bari and Taranto.

We'd already done a four week pre-jumping toughening-up course - mock jumping from platforms and trucks, run-marches, rock climbing, roping down the sides of ten- storey apartment blocks and, on the last day, the boxing tournament. It had stuck out a mile that Wally and I would be paired; we were much of a size, around 120 lbs, and the only officers on the course. So I'd put the best possible face on it and put my name down opposite his with dark threats that I was ready to wipe out his memories of Gib, India and Spain. In the event he was very kind to me, allowing me almost an even first round and a gentle minute of the second with lots of fancy slapping to make it look good. I never knew how it ended; someone was propping me up on the corner stool and dashing water over me as I gripped the ropes to stop the world going round. Well I suppose its not everyone who has been knocked out in the boxing ring - put it down to experience and soldier on.

That wasn't quite the end. The jumping was yet to come, slow pairs out of an aperture in Wellingtons, then fast pairs. Threes out of Hudsons, slow 18s out of C47s, fast 18s, full equipment fast 18s, and so on. Just the two jumps each morning before breakfast. Wally and I had half the course each, eighteen in number. we'd finished the aperture jumps, and the second jump this particular morning was to be our first out of Hudsons. While Wally was gossiping with me on the runway his Hudson opened up and roared off without him. He jumped in with me and when we looked down at his Hudson ten minutes later it was just a blazing mass on the edge of the D.Z. no survivors! Just three crew and seventeen trainees to bury a couple of days later, our Jack Battersby among them. They'd just spun in - no chance. A week later we stitched the brand new parachute wings on our sleeves, with just the odd stray thought on the way a spinning penny falls.

Spring was in the air and the Krauts retreating into the Po valley. The air was full of rumours of forthcoming attractions. One fine morning Brigadier Pritchard and I perched ourselves among the rocks on the northern slopes of the Appenines looking down over the enemy occupied Lombardy plain stretching lazy and blue into the distance towards the wall of the Alps. Far away the sun glinted on the flood waters of the great river. Our maps were strewn about us, corners held down by rocks as we considered various airborne landing possibilities. "You know, Turner," said the Brig brushing the flies away, "They're doing exactly the same in England at this moment, only they are fifty feet underground beneath the Green Park and pretty little girls are pushing tiny model aircraft and tanks across acres of maps, and generals by the dozen are breathing down their necks. We've a lot to be thankful for!" and he leaned back, stretching in the mid-day sun.

And so our successive plans were made and remade. Twice I got as far as sitting in my C47, lugging my homing beacon, as I awaited take-off, along with a score of other black-faced comedians, while the Bosch retreated towards the Alps. So in the end we never got that last operation and I never tried out my Pathfinder bit. There came an evening, as we had a glass of wine in the town, we noticed an unusual excitement about. The war was ending tomorrow, the Italians said. *"Guerra finira domane!"* they assured us and of course they were right. Next day it was official; the Germans in Italy had surrendered.

That evening stands out in my memory more clearly than yesterday. The tented camp in the olive grove, outside San Severo, quiet in the warm spring sun, lizards sleepy, crickets chirruping, rifle shots and tracer arching up over the town. The others had gone, just Wally, John and I in the mess tent, sitting silent, their thoughts probably the same as mine. No high jinks. It was over. Six years back and forth, up and down, over sea, over land and it was over, finished -

> Gentlemen rankers out on a spree,
> Damned from here to eternity.
> God have mercy on such as we.......

Names of friends drifted on the mind, places, those air-raids in Blighty: it seemed a generation ago. Dicing in Tiger Moths over the White Horse Downs. The convoys to Africa. The poor old Sherwood Foresters at Medfez-el-Bab where Tony Bracchi was killed and Jimmy Molloy. Sicily and all those chaps dropping down into the black sea, miles from land; not a hope. How long in the darkness had hope kept them swimming towards that impossibly distant shore? and all those others at Athens and Cassino, Taranto and Le Muy; that burning pyre at Gioya. Wendy Little, of Indiana, wishing us luck at Bari and Johnnie Davies, of Texas, trying to charm those expensive lovely floozies at Algiers into a cut-price job for the limeys. Bill Needle of New York looking down beside me into the fearful fiery crater of the erupting Vesuvius. The crash at Gela and the tow-rope failure in the middle of the Med, eighty miles out from Bizerta. Wally and I under arrest at Algiers and again that other time inside the fortress of Gib. The face of that girl at Cannes, watching the head-shaving of her friends in the town square; the screeching matrons, the porky, self-righteous Maquis. Rubbish! Gallant George Trippos and his friends at Megara, marvellous men and women, salt of the earth. The lady who lodged and fed us at Petrovac giving me a tub-bath, waving goodbye as we flew away, bending over her needles to wait for whatever the Germans might bring. Whatever happened to her was over long ago, water under the bridge now. God forgive us all that is past.

We stirred ourselves eventually and tried to put up a bit of a show, pretending to be tipsy, blazing away with our revolvers, but we had no heart for it. I think we were in bed before midnight, too old to cry ourselves to sleep.

Just a few days later I got orders to proceed as advance party to Naples and thence to Fargo Camp, Salisbury Plain, England, home and beauty. We embarked on the fine ship *Empress of Scotland* in the shadow of Vesuvius and came to anchor ten days later off Liverpool on Derby Day 1945. I put £10 on *Dante* and won £35: I was drinking his health at Fargo the next day and the day following, on my way Home.

Chapter 9
Home briefly, then off
To Palestine

It was getting on for tea-time as I arrived at Langwith. Grace was looking out for me and it was a happy homecoming though we must have felt a little strange with each other at first. Alan, three years old, straight faced and uncompromising, was not too sure of this stranger, but Chris on all fours was all smiles, happily darting about the floor like a crab in a pool. George was out on the farm somewhere and Beth was awaiting Allan's return from the day shift at Glapwell Pit. They had a flag flying from the clothes-post when we went to Palterton, which mystified me until Mother explained. - "It's for you of course, you chump!" Arthur said hello and Dad took me down to the Nags Head for an hour.

When the excitement had died down things were not so straightforward. George wanted to get married immediately and take over Bassett Farm on his own: he worked it within the month. Allan had bought 40 acres of land at Stockley and he and Beth were moving up to live at the Hall where Allan would work full time on Hall Farm, running his own little farm in his spare time. All of which left no job for me and no place for my family to live. It was not the homecoming I'd expected. I'd looked forward to getting back to the farm and had seen myself expanding the place with Arthur with whom I'd always got on better than anyone had. Well no one made any such suggestion and I didn't see myself asking. Truth to tell I suppose, to the family I was not the same person who had left the place in 1939. The Army had changed me, given me a second education, broadened my horizons; I'd held my own in a world beyond the limits of their imagining. So I whistled and went. There were no harsh words but it was obviously a load off my father's mind when I went back at the end of my disembarkation leave and rejoined the Squadron, signing on for an extra year, due to finish October '46.

We set up house for the time being, at Kingsdon in Somerset. Grace's sister Mabel and her husband, Arthur, rented a very pleasant cottage in the middle of the village. It was large by rural standards, four up and four down, two separate side by side cottages that had been joined into one. A stand pipe at the roadside a yard or two from the front door supplied our water and there was no electricity or gas. All the same it was roomy, weather-tight, and it was Grace's home village, even if twenty years and more had gone by since she had left when her parents died.

Back with the Squadron, we were billeted at the Balmer Lawn Hotel at Brockenhurst where we were in the height of luxury by our standards. The war was still going on and we daily expected to receive our orders for the Far East. However, along came the atom bombs and it was finally done with, in mid August - I've forgotten the date. I'd now rented a nice detached cottage in the New Forest about six miles away and a mile or two from Beaulieu, so we moved away from Kingsdon to our first separate home. There was a fine garden for the boys and a gardener included in the rent one day each week; the rent was £12 a month.

Failing the Far East, they had found another trouble spot brewing in Palestine and I found myself rejoining the 1st Airborne Division as 2nd I/C F. Squadron, and so I came to a final parting with the good old First Independent. At this distance of time you'll think it odd that I should still entertain a sentimental regard for the 'old mob'. I will only say that when you have been in such a company, over a long time, over great distances, in hazardous conditions of war-time soldiering, when we all had nothing except ourselves to depend upon, then if you were lucky you could reach heights of selfless companionship that had no parallel in normal daily life, a devotion that is indescribable, especially to women. It was a unique experience, never to be forgotten.

My first job was to get the new squadron embarked and complete with all equipment, stores and transport, and get it disembarked equally complete at the other end. That's one of the main jobs of a 2nd I/C and since I was reckoned more experienced than most, I was on my mettle and, no doubt, difficult to live with while it lasted. A tower of strength was Mick Briody who had been R.S.M. at Fargo when we were all training. He'd been in the Sicily and Arnheim landings and was now Lieut. Quartermaster. He was a grand fellow, a big ex-Irish Guards drill sergeant, and one of the very best. It was an uneventful voyage; if you except the time I won the last Housey-Housey pool, about £20, as we were arriving off Port

Said, and Mick and one or two others held me by my ankles, head down over the stern, until I promised to spend it all in drinks for everyone in the mess.

We fetched up, in late February '46 at Quassassin, on the Sweet Water Canal, half way between Cairo and Ismailia on the Suez Canal, and once more I had a great stroke of luck: well twice over. First my O.C., Freddie Aston, disappeared back home, never to return, and I became O.C. on my own once more. Secondly, while five of the six squadrons were sent up straight away to Palestine, my squadron was ordered to R.A.F. Kabrit on the Great Bitter Lake, to supervise the assembly and test flying of the Horsa gliders that were arriving there in crates and delivering them to the Div. H.Q. at Lydda in Palestine. It was grand to be on my own again and we passed a very pleasant summer. The R.A.F. assembled the Horsas, about fifty of them. As Chief Test Pilot, I flew each one, first time off the ground, passing it on to the rest of the squadron to be put through a thorough test-flight programme. It was not too strenuous even if a little dicey occasionally. Every afternoon we sunbathed or swam in the buoyant waters of the Lake, or joined the R.A.F. assembly crews who managed to turn out as many sailing dinghies as gliders! The Canal was very busy with troop-ships coming home from the East, and we had great fun beating them up as we showed off in the gliders. As we passed each one out, a crew came down from Lydda to collect it. There was just one casualty and that, right at the end of the summer, almost the last of them. We put his Horsa through its paces as usual and they came to fetch it. Unfortunately it never arrived at Lydda. Somewhere over the Sinai it just blew apart, a total casualty, almost certainly on account of turbulence.

Early morning flying out over the Eastern Desert was a never ending delight. The unchanging clarity of the sunrise revealed below ever changing shades of brown, red, yellow, grey, changing by the minute like shot silk in the wind, the heavens a limitless inverted glass of champagne. But it had another face; absolutely barren of vegetation, it began to take on, for me, something of the brooding menace of a sleeping giant. The fascination was tinged with respect. I found myself increasingly irritated by details that at one time I would have dismissed without a thought. An unscheduled inspection that found crews were not taking the trouble to check flight water reserves set me on edge. All the more so when I began to feel my colleagues were looking at me rather oddly as if the Old Man had better be quietly humoured.

By the end of August our job at Kabrit was done and we were soon due to move up to Division in Palestine. All good things come to an end. Years ago I made up my mind that the next boom location for the package holiday business would be the shores of Lake Timrah and the Bitter Lakes, Geneifa, Fanara, Fayid, Shandur and Kabrit. Well it hasn't happened yet so there are millions still to be made! It's a marvellous dry climate, and we sunbathed, unprotected, day after day with the shade temperature over a hundred Fahrenheit. Before we went I decided on one more little unofficial outing I'd had in mind for some time. On the excuse of a long-range reconnaissance exercise, we took two 15 cwt. trucks, a bowser and twelve men carrying all the water and stores, to make our way, via Suez, Aquaba and the Wadi Araba, to Petra and back. In the footprints of Lawrence of Arabia! The bowser took 200 gallons of water and we reckoned twelve days maximum for the trip, would have the rolling Desert of Tip to the north, with the coastal plain lost in the far northern haze. South would be the trackless red cliffs and gorges of the Jebel el Tip and south again the twin fingers of the Gulf of Suez and the Gulf of Arabia.

Three days over empty upland hard desert got us to Eilat. Turning north towards Petra, up the arid rift valley, we had little over a hundred miles to go but the going was very rough and there was much doubling back and forth as we came on impassable ravines and wadis. We had taken to night travel under the brilliant moon to keep both ourselves and our engines cool. Two nights and twenty hours of grinding away found us making camp and getting our heads down to catch the best of the sleeping time in the cool of the dawn, when the guard woke me to say that horsemen were approaching. The half-dozen Arabs arrived with a flourish, their leader in review order, the first rays of the peeping sun flashing on the jewelled hilt of the short curved sword in his belt, magnificently mounted and looking down his hooked nose at me with a disdain I recognised from long ago when, as a boy, I had run to throw open a field gate for a lady rider to the Rufford Hunt. He had a Sandhurst cultivated voice to match. Who were we? Did we know we were in Jordan territory? Where were we bound?

Well, we had only the vaguest idea where we were, and when he had showed signs of thawing down and even allowed his men to dismount and take a dish of coffee, he also dismounted, accepted a stiff tot of whisky against the morning chill, and listened to our story. "Petra? Why Petra? You're here! It's just down the Wadi there." It was only a cluster of dust filled ruins and holes in the cliffs, black in the morning shadows. We had to agree it didn't look much for all the trouble but at least we had got there. And having done so, he thought, on the whole, that our best course of action was to execute a smart about turn and make ourselves scarce before we became an international incident. He'd show us a short cut to the west to cut into the Beersheba-Ismailia road, but then he wasn't allowed across the border. No - better than the way we had come, and with an evil grin he was off and away. We set off back with the setting sun and, avoiding many of the detours we had marked, after four more arduous but eventful days we came out of the sands and looked down once more on Suez.

I was pleased. Wally should have been there, John would have got on with our Arab like a house afire, it was like the old days. The colonel nearly had a fit when he heard about it, thought I'd taken leave of my senses.

We went up to Palestine immediately: it wasn't for long, but long enough to learn what this newly coined word, terrorism, was about, long enough to learn that the Jews, from generations back, had forgotten more about guerrilla tactics than the Maquis, the Greeks and the Jugs had ever learned.

Still there remained one last tangle with fate! "You're a

jinx!" I had once been accused by Bill Needle and now I suddenly began to think there might be some thing in his claim. They had decided to show off the entire airborne outfit with a slap-up exercise, full scale. From Jerusalem, paras and gliders were to fly direct to Khartoum, do a landing demo for some general or other and then fly back. A thousand miles each way: setting off at first light we should, for the very first time in gliders, actually fly under the sun, directly under, in the peak of the day's heat. South of the sun, over the sea and desert with just a glimpse of the Nile, to sit down at Khartoum, at noon. They must be stark staring mad! Surely we'll be flying pretty high - as high as the R.A.F. decide! In the event it turned out to be a copy-book example of the ultimate Army cock-up!

Besides my co-pilot I had six airborne gunners, a jeep and an ammunition trailer and we arrived just about dead on noon. I'd had the gunners taking turns to hold a blanket over the pilot's head against the sun for the latter three hours overland, but in this non-stop Turkish bath I found myself sitting in two inches of my own sweat in the well of the bucket seat. Every glider arrived overhead so the R.A.F. had done their bit, but we lost six gliders in the landing. There was a very high wind and two turned turtle, one crashed, smashing the undercart and another landed on top of two that had already collided in landing. The general said it was excellent and I told my lot it was dreadful. Although they were all intact they were pretty scattered and it was nothing to brag about. The casualties I put down to exhaustion: in the relief of actually getting there they were so anxious to get on the deck that they lost their concentration.

The Paras landed in a high wind and were scattered all over the L.Z. with about thirty per cent casualties, four broken limbs and dragging abrasions; nearly as bad as Megara. There were no rocks here to be dragged over but the bone dry, dead flat gravel surface covered with tough dead looking thorn scrub was a terrible welcome for these paras who, up to now, had practised only on aerodrome grass.

We were due to take off again at first light for our return the following day, so what with manhandling the gliders for take-off at dawn, we had very little rest. However with the extra para casualties and one or two tow-ships requiring attention, it was late morning before all was set for take-off. In the short time available at the hurried planning stage of the exercise, I had already protested strongly against flying through the afternoon. Now surely the gliders at least should be held up for the following morning. At this date the sun here was dead overhead at noon, it was the hottest place on earth, the temperature about 130 F. Everybody knew the air could be rough enough to smash a glider to smithereens: we had lost one over the Sinai only a week or two back and two over Algeria back in '43. I was hurriedly and severely hushed! The general was there to see the whole shebang and that was that.

I was last away, tail-end Charlie, to see everyone airborne before I left. Someone had sent across a few odd bods when one of the C47s went u/s at the last minute so I had three extra passengers. The Nile in its great S-bend had left us to the east and, after getting on for two hours, back it came across our front and away to the west as we headed out over the Nubian desert, course slightly east of due north. We were being thrown all over the place, taking only ten minute spells at the controls, when there was a fearful thump. The Horsa checked speed, the tiresome rush of air dropped to a gentle rustle, the tow rope had gone! By the time I had checked to find it still dangling from the wing and realised it had come free from the Halifax, the latter had disappeared, and in all the wide sky, we were alone.

Below us on every side, as far as the eye could see, the rolling sandy and stony down-sized hills were empty of life. At least I'd had more than my share of forced landings already and this had no fears for me. It looked a piece of cake and so it turned out. We settled as merry as a bird, rolling no more than a hundred yards on hard sand.

Everybody out! swing the glider properly into wind and tie it down. The gunners, yellow under their tan with air-sickness, were only too glad to stretch their length on the ground in the shade of the wing. Sit back, take a deep breath and a little think. Surely we should hear the Halifax any minute coming back to look for us. course of action? - check water. There was a five gallon jerry can on the jeep and we had our own five gallons in the glider, several of the gunners had already drunk half their quart water-bottles before they landed. Eleven men; approximately 100 pints of water! I reckoned we were something like half way between Wadi Halfa on the Nile and

Port Sudan on the Red Sea; nothing showing on the map in the 300 miles between the two. Where was that damned Halifax? not a sign or sound. Course two - unload the jeep and trailer. No hurry, it would be cooler in an hour or two. The Halifax never came back. By four p.m. we had the jeep and trailer out and started up. I had a brief run to look for possible take-off room but when I'd got no more than a few hundred yards, the glider behind us melted into the mirage and disappeared! Back on our tracks and there it was again, but if we'd been gone an hour, in this wind, the tracks would be gone and we would never find our way back. About this time the sergeant and I began to look a bit strange at one another. The sun was sinking, massive and blood red. Time for another little think about tomorrow.

The wind had gone and the hiss of the blowing sand, not a sound! and then someone heard the tinkling bells. It was unbelievable at first but no doubt of it, coming out of nowhere! It was uncanny, hair-raising. While shepherds watched.....!! But no mistake, louder now, cow bells, and then suddenly, towering over us, a camel; then others, half a dozen and more. We had made our landing almost directly on a main caravan route between the Red Sea and the Nile. These coal-black Numidians must have watched the aerial armada flying by and, with delight, tracked down the fallen angel which was us. Stranded fliers were cash to them, golden sovereigns. These few were part of a great caravan of around forty camels whom we joined the following morning. We took the compass out of the Horsa and the Arabs loaded the jeep with spare blankets, axes, shovels and so on. They fashioned harness from the tow-rope and harnessed two camels to the jeep. By the time we got under way the Horsa had disappeared in the mirage and that was the last I heard of it.

It took us seven days non-stop travel to reach Wadi Halfa, footsore with marching, bum-sore from the wooden camel saddles, bearded, filthy, exhausted, we really welcomed the sight of the thin ribbon of green - no mirage this time - that marked the great river. We went down by River, Caique to Aswan and thence by train to Cairo. We had signed a paper for the leader of the caravan and I had thrown in the jeep for good measure.

Back at Div. H.Q. it was a nine-day wonder, bit of a joke really. Court of Inquiry? - well best not to rock the boat with the R.A.F. - all's well that ends well - best forgotten don't you think? - don't want to tread on anyone's toes, do we? - no point in stirring things up. You can put your crown up, that's something! Well, I thought; if that's it - bugger the Army! Within a month I was embarking at Port Said for Marseilles and on my way across France and the White Cliffs. Mid October 1946, with a new civvy suit and ten weeks final leave, I said goodbye to the Army for good.

After all the good times, the grand fellows, it was a pity it had to end like that. But I'd hung on too long. They were all gone - high time I followed them.

Chapter 10
Back to Family Life
-and Farming Again

I came home to lovely autumn weather at The Saeter, our old world cottage in the New Forest, to start being a full-time family man. For the first time I had to find someone to pay me a salary enough to keep four people housed, fed and clothed. Alan was just over four years old; mature for his years and very much the older brother of Christopher, just coming towards three. While I applied for various jobs, all associated with farming, the season turned to winter, the beginning of what was still remembered as the worst winter for generations. As I travelled here and there for interviews the snow grew deeper and deeper in the forest, There was a great national famine of fuel but we were lucky to be able to buy wood very cheaply and I spent days sawing logs and piling up a huge store in the conservatory.

One day I went off to see a London City banker in Fenchurch Street. He had advertised for an estate steward and farms manager. Mr. Brandt was quite impressive; old, must have been well into his seventies, grave of face, steely eyed, closely trimmed white beard, immaculately turned out in his dark city clothes, upstanding and active, he was obviously used to the deference which seemed to be showered on him.

"What would you do," he asked, "if you had a farm that was losing £10,000 a year?"

I was staggered. What sort of farm was this? I had to say something. "Off hand I've no idea," I said.

He sat back and fixed me with an eye like the Ancient Mariner and let me know that this was hardly the reply he'd expected of a serious applicant for the post he was offering, managing 600 acres in Surrey, 1200 in Oxfordshire and 500 in Berkshire, over 2000 in all! - and I'd been used to 120! I made haste to explain I didn't know exactly what I would do as such a thing was quite outside my experience. Amongst the farmers I had grown up with, no-one lost money, if you had a bad year you got rid of some men, pulled in your belt and worked harder and longer and eventually pulled through as we had all done in the early thirties. But £10,000, how could you lose that kind of money unless you were throwing it about like straw in the wind. Tomkins, the accountant, stirred in his chair and I don't think he ever really forgave me, but Mr. Brandt seemed pleased enough with my reply and I got the job, and so began my fourth education.

At first it all rather took my breath away. The only farmers I had known had working hands and muck on their boots and did their accounts on the back of used envelopes. Here in Surrey was the estate Steward with a fine house, two lady clerks in neat well-furnished offices with typewriters, filing cabinets and racks of account books. There was a farm manager, separate head herdsmen for the three herds of cattle, about 15 various farm workers, three farmsteads, twelve farm cottages, a laundry, a stud farm with groom and stableman, two estate maintenance staff and three gardeners. I would later find across the country in Oxford and Berkshire, four more farmsteads, forty men, thirty cottages and two more farm managers. I'd never seen a combine harvester in action but now we had four grand ones and two massive corn drying plants plus half a dozen assorted cars, vans and lorries.

It was March before we got settled in at The Stewards House, Capenor, with the months of ice and snow turning into floods everywhere. They've never reached those levels since then; there are lots of places where you can see marks painted up, *'Flood level, March 1947'*. The bitter winter was followed immediately by a glorious spring and summer and as the flood waters receded we were able to make a belated start on the sowing of the first corn crop. Mr. Brandt, though a merchant banker of several generations standing, had a keen appreciation of quality in animals, all his life he had keenly followed the hunt until the war put an end to it, he had owned some top class steeplechasers, one of which had twice run third in the Grand National. Since the horses had gone he had turned his enthusiasm to cattle and already had the best Sussex breed herd in the country - that first year we won the breed championship at the newly re-established Royal Show, our herdsman, Pat Sinclair, was one of the best and cleverest cattlemen in the country, a genius with beef cattle with generations of Scottish stockmen behind him. Now we started to build up herds of dairy cattle and, though they were far ahead in standard of any stock I had ever worked with, it would be a few years before they approached the class of our Sussex cattle. We had Ayrshire cattle in Surrey, a lovely breed of dairy cattle, Fresian dairy cattle at North Stoke in Oxfordshire and Hereford beef cattle at North Farm in Berkshire, around 300 head all told by the end of my first year. Perhaps I should make it clear that dairy cows are specialist milk producers; they are spare of body flesh and you could never fatten them. Beef cattle are bred for the butcher and only produce enough milk to feed their one calf each year.

The reasons for the poor results soon began to show themselves. We had good land, modern machinery and good cattle. The shortcomings were in management and labour. The slackness and ignorance was hardly believable and I soon realised that, in spite of the modest scale of my previous experience, the solid grounding in my father's standards carried a degree of solid farming capacity far ahead of these down here in the south, a level of work capability at least double that expected of farm workers here. In the first year, as a result of a discrepancy in a sack-hire invoice, I had to sack the North Farm manager who was selling corn for his own pocket, and in the second year I got rid of the Capenor man for general incompetence, putting Pat Sinclair in his place. Staff numbers gradually reduced and, developing my own eye for cattle, I was able to steadily increase and improve the dairy herd.

Mr. Brandt showed every confidence in me and I was left to run the sales and buying quite unhampered by supervision. All the same he was not generous with salaries; I had been glad to start at £450 per year and by 1950 it had gone up to £650. It doesn't sound much now but it was getting on for three times what the men got and we had many perks, free house, gas and electricity, free milk and vegetable produce, free car, free gardener so we were able to live at a comfortable standard. We were able to send the boys to a small but quite good private school, Hillsbrow, half way to Redhill - it was knocked down some years ago - where they charged a little over £100 a year for the two of them, dinners included. Grace and I shared the benefits of the school for we were regular supporters of the rugger and cricket teams and attendees at the Sunday morning chapel cum coffee and biscuits, making many lasting friendships among the other parents. They were mainly local professional and business people, quite a few Londoners and some from surprisingly far afield with one or two foreign importations. we knew all the staff very well and though none of them was qualified by today's criteria, together they ran a very attractive school. Miss Brown and Miss Wilson, sixty-ish, both of them, ran the juniors as a kind of old fashioned dame school with a quiet dignity and an obvious love of their work. No school subject was allowed to take precedence over the overriding importance of good manners. The headmaster had an instant and total command of discipline and the games coaching was on a vastly higher level than anything I had known in my own school days when games coaching was non-existent. Instead of a dull annual concert or Shakespeare play they put on a Christmas variety show of surprising standard, with the assistance of several parents with show business connections. One year they included my *Mumming Play,* which was, of course, unknown in Surrey. Altogether, Hillsbrow occupied quite an important influence in our lives during the first ten years of our lives in Surrey.

Chris had started at a little old-fashioned dame school run for a few village children by a Mrs. Crowe at her house in South Nutfield. She was Dutch by birth, quite unqualified, but a natural born teacher. An enthusiastic member of the W.I., she was one of those people who are skilled in any handicraft. Her two sons had been at Hillsbrow and had gone on to Blundell's School where Ted, the elder, eventually became a housemaster. Her husband had a comfortable job in the City as a tea broker; he was a cricket and rugby buff, running his own Sunday team throughout the summer and never missed an international match at Twickenham where I remember some great games in his company. We remained close friends until long after we'd left Surrey. They both died in the early seventies.

Another circle of friends was based on our farming neighbours. I got interested in the N.F.U. of which my grandfather had been a founder member seventy years before, and became chairman of the Redhill branch, serving on the county committee and at N.F.U. Headquarters in London. For people in the dairy and beef cattle business we were spreading the name of Capenor far beyond our county boundaries, entertaining buyers who had come half way round the world to see our cattle and ship them back to Texas, Kenya and South West Africa. My first overseas sale had been our champion bull of 1947 who had gone to Windhoek in South West Africa where he unfortunately died two years later, probably due to a shortage of trace elements in his diet; he had taken to licking the sand in those arid regions and had succumbed to the undigested accumulation in his stomach, but not before the buyer, a Mr Zogeiser had formed a very high opinion of him. Now it happened just then that we had the finest Sussex bull we ever produced who was the last and best of the progeny of Mr. Zogeiser's bull, and, hearing of this he decided to come over from Africa to see Capenor Cassius, as we had named the young sensation. Cassius had just won the supreme beef championship at the Royal Show and, sure enough, Zogeiser bought him, breaking all the price records for the Sussex breed. He was shipped out to Walvis Bay where there was no quay for ocean-going ships, and Cassius was slung out to be moved ashore by lighter. Struggling in his hemp harness at this alarming experience, Cassius fell out of the rope cradle into the shark infested waters, whereupon the assembled natives formed a protective crescent round him and swam him to the beach where he came ashore, none the worse for his adventure. We could claim, not only that he was exported to Africa for a record figure, but that he actually swam there! This story has a romantic footnote: Zogeiser had been in communication with a young lady in Germany who had survived the Jewish pogrom as an orphan girl; he went over to Germany and brought her back and they were married and, I'm sure, lived happily ever after!

Mr. Brandt had taken up steeplechasing again and we had occasional outings to Lingfield, Hurst Park, Sandown, Newbury and Kempton Park, and of course, Cheltenham. The farms were prospering, the boys doing well and these, I think, were the happiest days of our lives. Alan and Chris spent their weekends and holidays running wild with school friends in the woods that came right up to the garden fence and where they had a tree house from which to watch the rabbits, squirrels and foxes. There were badgers too that I had seen once or twice going out for an early morning rabbit for the pot. This was marred by Alan's serious accident when he was about nine years old. Playing on the high bank overhanging the Outwood Road, he slipped and fell in front of a car passing below. With a broken femur, arm and ribs and severe shock, he was critically ill for some days and spent the next four months in the East Surrey Hospital at Shaws Corner halfway between Redhill and Reigate. Mrs. Brandt, who was on the management committee of the hospital, was instrumental in getting him a private ward and seeing that he lacked for nothing in attention. He was home for Christmas but wore a calliper until Easter. He had been captain of the Junior XV but all this put an end to that kind of sporting activity. He did start boxing again and did very well, twice knocking out his opponent in the annual boxing competition: apart from swimming, it was the only sport he could take part in and he made the most of it.

Two things had us quietly worried. Mr Brandt was by now around 85, and, fit as he had always been, he could not last for ever. There was no sign from his sons of any interest in farming or that I should ever have the opportunity of taking over any of the land. Secondly, comfortable as we were, Mr. B. was not a generous man with salaries, and half the emoluments of the job for me were in the form of perquisites that went with the job. There was no prospect that we should be able to afford to send the boys away to school at the end of their days at

Hillsbrow as most of the other boys had done in the past. However Alan did so well in the 'eleven-plus' exam that he got a scholarship to Ottershaw, a Surrey County Council boarding school, where he stayed until he left school at 18 with excellent exam results that easily qualified him for university entry. He was not interested and anxious only to get a good job as soon as possible. This he did with Barclays Bank D.C.O. with a view to eventual posting overseas. Exams came easy to him, but not so school life in general which he hated. He made friends with like minded companions and indeed was lucky not to be expelled for bad behaviour generally. Chris got into Reigate Grammar School and struggled to get enough qualifications to get into a bank at Dorking. School work did not come easy but he made the best of it and was always cheerful, never short of friends, and altogether easier to get on with than Alan. He was keen on the Cadet Corps at Reigate and would have liked to get into the Army Officers School at Welbeck but his exam results were never good enough.

In the meantime the farms continued to prosper. We won all kinds of trophies and when we started sending Herefords to the annual Smithfield Show, we never once failed to win a first prize and this in competition with the best cattle in the country. The Milk Marketing Board published performance figures for the whole country in milk records and by 1955 we were top of the league for Ayrshires in the south east region. There were no clouds on the farming horizon.

At home in Derbyshire, Scarcliffe Grange Farm came up for

sale and we had a family conference to pool our resources. In the event Dad failed to buy it. He was underbidder at a ridiculously cheap price, but was nervous about remortgaging his land after spending a lifetime in getting clear of debt. We might have got it for £20,000. Fifteen years later it was worth nearly a million!

Then, one fine day in March, we had an outing to Cheltenham Races. Our horse, Noble Legend, was favourite to win the Grand Annual, the two mile 'chasing blue ribbon but Mr. B. was feeling off colour so I had to go to declare the runners. Poor Noble Legend! He never started to race, going straight through the first fence as if he was blindfold, and Mike Scudamore pulled him up long before the finish. As he came in he told me quietly, "They did us! Keep your fingers crossed - the stewards may want us." Well they didn't. They let it go but when I went over to Blenchingly House that evening, Mr. B. was horrified and very shaken. He had a stroke that night and never left his bed again; he died six months later. He was morally as straight as a dye; he often quoted his father who had died when he was a young man: - "Do the right thing and in the end it will be the profitable thing." As in the City, so in racing, without question you ride to win. The possibility that his horse had been in a fixed race killed him.

He was 87. His family had first come to England in 1812 and quite fortuitously at that. There was a Hamburg merchant who decided to send his two sons to Archangel to learn the timber trade and extend his existing interests there. Now we were at war with the newly born United States and these two young adventurers speculated on a couple of cargoes of timber to Charleston, running the blockade of the British Fleet. As luck would have it they were collared by the British and their ships impounded off the Isle of Wight and they were interned. The restrictions on their liberty however did not prevent them from seeing enough of the City of London to be very impressed by its status as the mercantile centre of the world. The little American war being soon over, their ships with their Charleston charter were released in 1813, but once clear of the Channel, undaunted by their earlier misfortune, they smartly eluded the Navy and doubled back to run into Bordeaux and conclude a lucrative deal with Bonaparte, quite sufficient, after Waterloo, to set them up in the business in the City of London as William Brandt's Sons and Company, Merchants of Fenchurch Street.

Mr. B. had, in the office safe, a beautifully finished, silver-plated Smith and Wesson pearl handled, six-shooter and one day I asked him about this revolver. It had been bought in Buenos Airies sometime about 1890. What he described as three young rakes, Rothschild, Hambros and himself, had gone out to look at progress on the railway their parents were instrumental in financing in the Argentine. To relieve a temporary boredom, they decided to ride across the continent, through the Andes, to see if they could reach the Pacific. Eventually reaching Santiago, he took the opportunity to set up an agency in Valparaiso for the guano trade. "I bought the revolver for the journey but never used it as far as I can recall," he explained. He had relatives all over Northern Europe for in spite of their English domicile, the men of the family were always educated in Germany and so tended to find their wives in Europe. His mother was Russian and his wife East Prussian. She outlived him by several years. His brother Rudolph had gone back to Russia in 1918 after the family estates had been overrun by the Bolsheviks and retrieved some of the family jewellery his mother's relatives had hidden when they fled from the revolutionaries. He was a bachelor and lived at Ruthin Castle in N. Wales. He happened to call at Capenor on the day the death was announced of Mrs. Keppell and the two octogenarians had a laugh together about *The Times* piece "Noted Edwardian Hostess". Mr. Brandt never mentioned any investment tips but he was a keen student of history and long before the resurgence of Germany and Japan as industrial powers, he once said, "My father always said, 'Lend your money to a beaten enemy'." He was very interested in my flying. Although in his youth he had driven a six-in-hand, he had never learned to drive a car.

I had joined the R.A.F.V.R. shortly after we came to Capenor. Having started, at my mother's suggestion, as a trooper in the Sherwood Rangers Yeomanry in 1933, when we still had horses, or more correctly, chargers, sabres and lances and when Mother's brother, Sid, was still Regimental Sergeant Major, I had had a variety of service in the volunteer forces. We had lost our horses in 1936 and became a signals unit, which did not suit me, so I joined the Sherwood Foresters as an infantryman. By 1938 we had become a search-light unit,

Royal Engineers, so I became a Sapper. At the outbreak of war we became Royal Artillery, but I never became a Bombardier as, by then, I had clawed my way up to the dizzy rank of Sergeant. Back in the Foresters as an infantryman Lieutenant in 1941, I transferred to the Airborne Force at its inception in 1942. So finding myself farming on the edge of Redhill Airfield, where they were forming the Volunteer Reserve, I thought it would be interesting to join the R.A.F. for a change and lost my Army rank of Captain to become a humble Pilot Officer.

We did 40 hours a year flying in Tiger Moths, Magisters and later, Chipmunks and I thoroughly enjoyed it until the V.R. was stood down five years later. I could take a couple of hours off, if the office was quiet, and park Grace and the boys on the edge of the field and spend the afternoon doing circuits or aerobatics, or even cross-country trips to see how the farming was getting on over in Oxfordshire and Berkshire. I once flew up to Wolverhampton, landing there and hopping a lift to the Royal Show at Shrewsbury, collecting the Sussex Cattle Champion trophy from the Queen, then thumbing my way back to my Tiger Moth at Wolverhampton and so home to Redhill to complete a full day. It was an incomparable experience on night flying practice, to fly in the open cockpit in the cool air of a midsummer night, solo over the lights of the South London suburbs and over the dark downs of Sussex.

On my very last day, bright, cloudless with unlimited visibility, I took up a Tiger Moth. We were not allowed to fly higher than

4,000 feet, but it was such a wonderful day that I climbed and climbed until I reached 12,000 feet and felt quite light-headed as I looked over the side at the panorama below. Westward, I could see Portsmouth harbour with Spithead and the Isle of Wight beyond; north-west sprawled the whole of London and north-east, the sand flats and marshes of Essex and Suffolk up towards Ipswich. To the east, beyond the shores of Kent, the islands of the mouth of the Rhine dappled the sea, leading my eyes down past Dunkirk and down past Le Touquet toward Abbeville and Dieppe. What a sight! But I felt rather uncomfortable knowing I was breaking flying rules and was in the track of civil airlines flying in to Heathrow, so I turned on a long glide for home, but I was glad I'd made it a day to remember as I touched down for the last time and taxied up to Redhill Tower and got out of my straps, pushing back my goggles and slipping the button of my leather helmet.

Helicopters took our place on the airfield. I had met Alan Bristowe at the N.F.U. meetings where he had rather an abrasive effect on the conservative ideas of the stolid Surrey farmers, and got to know him better the night he'd taken delivery of a brand new £30,000 Rolls-Royce but got so tipsy he dared not drive it and asked me to drive him home to Fortune Farm at Leigh. His father had set up a pre-war flying school at Cambridge, passed it over, profitably, to the R.A.F. for the duration, and young Alan became an ace test pilot as might have been expected from his notably extrovert character. Reluctant to admit that the war was over, he turned, in 1947/8 to gun-running and surplus arms dealing in the Indonesian revolution and made a lot of money. He had tried whale hunting with a helicopter-mounted harpoon gun and by the time the Korean war came along he had made himself a corner in helicopters and a millionaire into the bargain. He'd gone in with Freddie Laker in the formation of British United Airways but they were too similar in character to work in harmony, so back went Bristowe to his helicopters, part of his enterprise being the score or so machines on which the Navy were now training at Redhill.

One day he drew up beside me outside the farm gate to pass the time of day and, finding me preoccupied, wanted to know what was biting me. I explained that I'd lost a sheep! There should have been 50 but after repeated searching we could only find 49. "Get in!" he said and within a couple of minutes we were sliding to an impressive standstill on the airfield apron. Up the tower steps he shot into the Chief Flying Instructor's office. "Bristowe," he said, "These are my helicopters." He waived towards the windows. "This is my friend, Mr. Turner." Within five minutes he'd persuaded the C.F.I. that his bored pupils, doing circuits and bumps, would be better off doing far more useful training by finding my missing sheep. Within the hour the air over Henhaw Farm was full of helicopters hovering like gnats on a summer evening, and they found my sheep which had slipped into a deep, briar-overgrown ditch. I often wondered how much that sheep cost the tax-payer. Bristowe was delighted. He needed no thanks; it simply delighted him to show off his muscle and he could certainly do that. I did not however fancy becoming his farm manager! Since then of course, he has gone from strength to strength with a monopoly of the servicing of the North Sea oil rigs, and doubtless in any other part of the world's oceans where they drill for oil. A man and a half? More than that!

There was no sign from the sons of their carrying on with the farms although Mr B. had mentioned several times in recent months that the price of land was due for a substantial rise. They simply had no interest in the land and animals which had, all his life, absorbed so much of their father's affections. No, it was a case of selling up the lot as soon as taxation factors would permit. I had hoped I would be given the opportunity of a tenancy of some of the Surrey land if they did not want to keep it in hand, but there was no hope, and the sons were determined to get out of land completely.

Agreement on the valuation for death duties dragged on for month after month. There were important cattle sales to arrange. The farm sales involved detailed preparation of catalogues. With one thing and another, it was three years before the job was done and the executors were ready to give me six months notice. There was no golden handshake, no pension. I had appreciative letters from the livestock auctioneers and from the agents for the land sale but from the family, nothing.

The boys had left school during this period of limbo and were at work. Alan had passed his A level G.C.E. in all three subjects, with distinction in French, but he did not want to go to university and said he wanted to start work immediately. We did not try to change his mind. Although he seemed to be able to pass exams at will, his school reports on general behaviour were not good and it seemed best to let him get to work if that was what he wanted. Chris had struggled to get four O level passes but managed to get a job in the bank. At any rate they were both started and at a pinch could look after themselves.

It was just as well for I found, at 50, that the country was full of young budding farm managers with all sorts of university degrees. I made dozens of job applications and wandered all over the country from one interview to another with depressing lack of success. My practical experience indeed was not always to my advantage. If the truth be told I suppose I was pretty full of myself and did not go down well at some of these interviews. The fact that Mr. B's death had left me without a reference did not seem to matter as much as I had thought. Eventually I took a job, east of Hull, with a go-getting trawler owner who was about to set the farming world alight. It lasted just five weeks before I took the first opportunity, just after Easter 1963, of shaking the slush of Yorkshire off my feet. Grace and I had the final experience of storing all our furniture, getting into our laden Hillman one spring morning and pointing it down the Great North Road not knowing where we would sleep that night or where in the world our future lay, and so we came to leave Capenor. We had had seventeen good years there, made good, civilised friends: interesting, successful work in marvellous country surroundings in which the boys had grown up and which we were sure they would remember all their lives. For Grace and I, those were the happiest years but the chapter had come to an end, and somewhere, unknown to us, a new one had to be started.

Well, what an upset it turned out to be. I was determined not to go anywhere near Palterton as we pointed the Hillman southwards, and we fetched up that afternoon at a caravan site in the village of Gunthorpe, on the Trent, about ten miles east of Nottingham. We got ourselves set up very comfortably. The site was the orchard of an old farmhouse and the owner was a queer old biddy of fifty or sixty, a Miss Houghton. A small world they say! This Miss Houghton was the daughter of J.P.Houghton who had been Chairman of the Bolsover Company when I had been there before the war, a very prominent industrial leader, credited by some as being one of the chief architects of the smashing of the great coal strike of 1926. As a girl she had known Elms Farm at Palterton when my grandfather lived there and was sure there must be some family connection since his second Christian name was the same as her family name and very unusual at that. He had always called himself Cornelius Houghton although his grandfather's gravestone at Ault Hucknall spelled it Hufton. At all events she made us very welcome. After a few weeks, during which I helped my cousin, Theo, with the accounts of his building business at Barnstone, just a few miles south of the river, I landed the job of farm manager at Silverstone motor racing circuit. Well, glamorous as it sounded, it was a great disappointment; it was very isolated and Grace was very lonely, though she did start to learn to drive round the track. I could not get on at all with the General Manager and after two months we gave up and repacked our traps. A phone call to Miss Houghton told us our van was still available so back we scooted to Gunthorpe and how glad we were to be back.

It was now August 1963 and I had decided, after so much disappointment, to leave farming alone and see if I could get some other kind of work. Since we had to have a house, we decided to buy a small detached village shop nearby at Radcliffe-on-Trent and in no time at all Grace was presiding there as if she'd been there for years. Almost immediately I got a general clerical job at the Gas Board at Nottingham and, a month or two later, a better one as auditor with a firm of chartered accountants. Then, out of the blue, came a reply from an application I'd put in and forgotten about some time before. It was with the Central Electricity Generating Board at Birmingham as Way-Leave Officer. This was strange country indeed and not at all to Grace's liking, but financially it was attractive and I decided to give it a go, travelling daily the 120 mile return journey. As things turned out, it was the best move we've ever made. By 1 Feb 1964 I was at work in a strange city, a year almost to the day since leaving Surrey. It had been a rum year too, bundled about from pillar to post, sometimes discouraged, but always trying something; and now it seemed there was a brighter horizon once more, even if it was in the assembled native place I had always associated with grime and smoke and blast-furnaces - the Black Country - what a name to be saddled with!

The reality was something different. A great city, booming with reconstruction; huge civil engineering projects, busy people swaggering in their prosperity; house building and house demolition at a frantic rate; everybody working, everybody spending. What a town - all that industry, a buzzing in the air, a sense of power spreading like a contagion. By contrast, South London seemed a down at heel collection of worn-out property, and much of it, from the river to Streatham and from Tooting to Millwall remains to this day. I'm biased of course. I'd only been there a few days when I drove out one frosty morning to Frankley Beeches, 700 feet up on the south west city boundary. The sun was well up and you could see 20 miles clear across the city to the bandstand on Barr Beacon, 800 feet on the northern heights and in between the great sprawl of the city as clear as crystal. I fell for 'Brum' that day, and though these twenty years have all left their scars on 'The City of a Thousand Trades', its day will come again. They are that kind of folk.

After a year's house negotiation worry, we were settled here in Solihull, and if you have to live in a town, you'd travel the length of England to find one better! We were lucky in our final choice of location and never regretted it.

From the start I enjoyed my work with the Central Electricity Generating Board. It was to do with the network of high-tension connections from the great power stations ringing the city into local sub-stations that, in turn, distributed the power to railways, industry, streets and houses. Business in the early 60s was expanding at a phenomenal rate and we were erecting giant towers and burying miles of cable at a feverish pace. In hind sight, I suppose those days had much in common with the height of the Roaring Twenties boom before the crash of the Great Depression of 1929.

Wherever a line was strung or a cable buried, it was necessary first to get permission of the local authorities and every owner or occupier of every yard of land involved. That written permission agreement was called a Way-Leave, and getting it all signed, sealed and delivered was my job as Way-Leave Officer. We were up against all kinds of opposition, from worthy bodies like The Society for the Protection of Rural England, to whom we appeared to be vandal destroyers of the amenities of the countryside, to spluttering farmers brandishing their guns or holding back their hounds! Once in construction, I had to see that minimal damage was caused and that it was fairly recompensed by the Board and by the contractors.

The contractors, Irishmen all, were a tough bunch, but this side of the business was right up my street - how Alan would have enjoyed it - and I quickly established myself as a keen negotiator. Free lunches galore were to be had in the hope of a favour here and a blind eye there, but they soon tailed off when they paid no dividends. This smart-Alec approach was new to me and I soon realised that the morality of the farming world was something quite apart from this. In this city, in our industry alone, tens of millions of pounds worth of construction contracts were being handed out by quite modestly paid municipal or public utility engineers, and the same was true of Gas coming in from the North Sea and house building. The temptations were obvious, especially for men who had grown up in the wide-boy, city-slicker atmosphere in which I now found myself.

The easy-going attitude of some of my colleagues left me cold. I had grown up to be frugal to excess, always wanting value for money and delighting in hard, harsh negotiation just for the fun of it. In the Army I had learned quite a deal about men. At Capenor, Mr Brandt, as straight as a dye himself, had given me trust as a natural right. My farming experience had given me a keen eye for a plausible rogue and a sensitive hand for a flatterer. It is not in the least surprising that the low calibre of supervision skill and cost consciousness have produced monuments of civil engineering, badly planned, dishonestly or incompetently built and already, in less than a generation, beginning to fall to pieces.

It all got my back up and set me all the more determined to see the job well done. It did me no harm. Although I had started at almost 51 years old, I soon got myself marked and quickly improved my position. The secretary urged me to complete my Chartered Institute of Secretaries studies - I had left my finals half done in 1939 - as there was still promotion available. Well, I did not take his advice. I doubted if my brain could cope with that sort of study at my age and anyway, in spite of its difficulties, or because of them, I liked my way-leave job too much.

Happy as our days at Capenor had been, I came to see how circumscribed they had been for me, spending seventeen of my best years too effortlessly and cosily cocooned in that comfortable life. How often I wished I had got out years before especially when I looked round me at the very ordinary calibre of some of my seniors. But I loved every day of the cut and thrust of the job, so much so that, in the course of time, I began to look forward with horror to my approaching retirement. It had been a strange sequence of jobs and events and travels that had brought me full circle, so close finally to the surveying I had started straight from school in 1930.

When the awful day arrived, 4th March 1968, I could not bring myself to give up work with a good grace. I got myself a ganging job on the gardening staff at the National Exhibition Centre and strung it out to the November before giving it up for the winter. I was not to know then that it was for good and that my health would so adversely affect the next few years.

Chris had got married in 1965 and Alan a year later. We weren't very keen on Alan's Jill. I think she was his first experience of girls - those damned boys schools have a lot to answer for - and she made all the running to the wedding day. They never settled down however and we were not surprised when they separated very soon. There was to be a divorce at the earliest possible date we understood but for some reason unknown to us, progress in that direction was nil. Chris, on the other hand, got on marvellously with Val right from the start.

After flirting with insurance he went back to banking and got himself happily established with the National Westminster in London. Tracy and Michael added to their responsibility in 1966 and 1969 while they were still living in Torquay.

Alan also had a false start or two but before long got a job in Croydon selling cars with a good firm. It suited him down to the ground and he looked set for a lucrative career. He sometimes called to see us as he ferried cars back and forth and always had money in his pocket. By now he had met Amanda and set up house in Surrey, his first independent home, by the time Caroline came along in 1971. He and Amanda being both at work, they brought her up to us (at six weeks old), and for the best part of six months we were *in loco parentis* again. Well hardly 'again' for me as I had missed all the babyhood of our boys during the war and it was a new experience. How we enjoyed it too and it was a hard day for us when they decided to have her back. They got on very well and all went down to Torquay for a holiday summer. Then, without warning, the blow fell and their lives together were at an end. Amanda had brought Caroline up to us for a day or two and Alan was to follow for the weekend. But it was the police who arrived to tell us he had taken his own life, at Nutfield, his childhood home.

So Amanda and Caroline were on their own and Caroline just one year old. It was an awful position for Amanda but, to her eternal credit, she faced it with unflinching courage, getting Caroline into a day-nursery and setting out to reshape their lives. Luckily, the firm had Alan well insured and eventually, although his marriage to Jill had never been dissolved, I was able to persuade the trustees of the scheme that Amanda was the proper person to get the benefit. They were thus able to buy their little old world cottage at Howard Road, Reigate.

Val and Chris had added Richard to their family in 1972, not without serious difficulty as far as Val was concerned. The tiny infant spent his first few weeks in Carshalton hospital and only urgent surgery within an hour or so of his birth kept him going. He's all right now, still small but fit and sharp as any of them. Alan seemed to have been a bit of an afterthought when he came along in 1979. He is a strong lad, already making his presence felt in the growing family around him.

Caroline, I have to confess, has been a bit of a favourite with me from the start. I can only plead that, lacking a father, she has had a strong claim to special attention. She seems to have enjoyed her stays with us in all the school holidays. She has shown the same courage as her mother who has made such a good job of her upbringing. She has an engaging personality, intelligent, bright, eager and conversational to a degree less evident with Chris' family with their less extrovert character. She is doing very well at school and I think, has already shown the resource to do as well in life. Of course we realise that we have by now, in all probability, already seen the happiest of our times with the older of them and Caroline, on the threshold of her teens, has horizons opening to her in which we shall have no part. No matter, it is her life and, with love, we wish her and the others the best of fortune.

Father had died quietly at Hayes Farm near Ashbourne on 14th June 1970. He and mother had moved there to live with Beth and her family following his retirement. Although Arthur had been, in effect, running the farm for several years, he had kept himself busy with his sheep and a few light jobs as long as he was able. He had been forced to finally retire in 1963 when he lost his sight, suddenly, as a result of a stroke and handed the farm enterprise at Palterton Hall to Arthur, with Ellen and her large family moving into the house to look after him. Dad and Mother had been an undemonstrative couple after the northern fashion but, in fifty-nine years of marriage, unstinting frugality, good health, above average intelligence and plain hard labour had built the most successful farm undertaking for miles. Dad was universally respected in farming circles and much loved in the family. They were both a strong advert for the skill of the late Victorian village school teachers who had taught them up to their fourteenth birthdays, Dad was always ahead of me in mathematics, well beyond matriculation standard, and an avid reader of history and geography. Mother was a highly skilled letter writer, meticulous in grammar as well as calligraphy, and of a standard of composition quite beyond current 'O' level.

My brother, Arthur, died 29th March '81, ten days after his 69th birthday. He had never been ill since boyhood, never worn glasses and never been to a dentist. Farming had been his whole existence, his whole life devoted to proving that he could work better, faster and for longer hours than anyone else in sight. Painfully shy with girls, I don't think he ever let them into his life. Even in his own home he would not join in any visiting company and rarely moved beyond the kitchen and his simple hardwood chair. He enjoyed preparing the barn for summer barn dances (Ellen had one or two charity do's) but never showed his face on the night. He spent many hours decorating the whole farmstead with bunting for the Silver Jubilee, but only so that he could - and did - win first prize in the village. Of course, I only saw him, after 1939, for short periods of a day or two at a time but I got on very well with him and we often went for long walks together on Sundays or summer evenings. He was trapped in the loneliness he had himself fostered all his life and eagerly grasped the chance of companionship and quiet country talk. But he could never suffer fools, nor opposition in argument, nor failure to get his own way and his fiery temper, when in danger of being crossed, was known and fearfully respected far and wide. He had not bought a suit for twenty years, but the farm valuation he left to his two nephews, Robin and Timothy, was close on four hundred thousand pounds, every penny of it to them and their mother, Ellen.

Mother outlived him by a year, passing quietly away 28 February 1982 at Hayes Farm, near Ashbourne, where Beth had looked after her devotedly since she left Palterton in 1963. To the end she was a miracle of health, though increasingly frail at 94, she was able to get about the house, read sensibly and exercise her own opinions intelligently and forcefully. Sadly she and Arthur were too much alike to get on with each other and scarcely spoke for over twenty years till the day he died. She was latterly much occupied with the past and enjoyed maintaining a busy correspondence with the Muirs and their long families scattered about Australia with all the snippets of family that came to mind. Like her father, she was an accomplished letter writer and was quietly pleased when she had one published in the *Derbyshire Countryside,* setting the editor right as to the correct way pegged hearth rugs had been made a century before.

She was very highly regarded in a very extended family circle, but nearer at hand occasional flaws were to be seen. Her strict exercise of authority, harsh sometimes, over her children up to their marriages and beyond (shades of her aunt, Maria Muir) was not always excusable. Like Arthur, she would not be crossed. This did not apply to Grace and I who were protected by distance and, after all, I had been independent of my parents since 1939 and an odd one out sometimes before that. She left her little fortune to be divided equally between her fourteen grandchildren. Beth, who had selflessly watched over them both from hour to hour for twenty years received not a penny - and, incidentally, in the whole family carve up, neither did I.

And there our history comes to an end, Grace and I finding ourselves at the allotted span, as they used to say. We are very comfortable here at Solihull were it not for the distances separating us from our families. Still we see Chris and his lot several times a year, either here or in Kent. I quite enjoy our once or twice a year drives to Palterton, not so much at seeing

CORNEY AND GRACE 1981.

my sister's family, as for the local walks and memories, and the runabouts looking up cousins and friends in the village and at Heath, Tibshelf, Bolsover, Chesterfield, Nottingham and Derby. There are whispers that the Sprays [*Ellen and family*] have half a mind to sell the Hall and the morality of such an idea, in view of the way it came to them, leaves me speechless. Caroline and Amanda of course we see every holiday. Amanda seems increasingly prosperous; we would have liked her to have found another partner but there are no signs that way. Caroline remains what she has been since we first set eyes on her, a shining light in our lives.

We have put much of ourselves into our house and garden here and I try to keep at bay the nagging feeling that we shall, sooner or later, have to give it up. Years do weigh ever more heavily and health is no longer taken for granted so we enjoy these quiet later years of a wonderful partnership that has never known a false step.

The sorrows and hardships of Grace's early years helped to build a towering strength of purpose and a capacity for love and thoughtfulness that have sustained her beyond measure all her life.

There were hard times in our youth for all our generation but at least they gave you the chance to feel your strength, through years of rewarding work and lasting friendships. For me there were also those selfishly adventurous years of war with unforgettable comrades, a good fairy always at my shoulder over deserts, mountains and seas, through the most heart stopping and breath-catching and fulfilling times. What luck that, on that very last evening of peace in 1939, I first met Grace at North Cave, luck that has blessed us, in such generous measure, with good fortune all our days. To any of our grandchildren who may read these words we have to admit that all our dreams did not come true and we never set the world afire. Nevertheless, if they are lucky enough to come out faring no worse, they will have much to be thankful for in the end.

Chapter 11

Postscript

The forgoing memories were written in 1983 and unfortunately my father never added to them during the ensuing years. Although I have not inherited my father's gift for narration, I feel I must make a humble effort to add the final chapter to the story, to tie up any loose ends and to fill in a few details of the last few years of his life.

Shortly after he finished the writings, his sister Beth, of whom he speaks so fondly, having lost her husband, Allan, in the spring of 1983, decided to go on a trip to Australia to visit her daughter and family now that she no longer had her mother to look after. She had never travelled outside the country before and, sadly it was to be her one and only trip. She died on the aircraft during the journey home. A lovely natured person, so different from most of the family, her passing was another blow to Dad following so soon after his mother and brother, Arthur.

His worst fears about Palterton Hall were realised. That great rambling house which so dominated the hill-top village, looking down on his beloved Doe Lea Valley spread out below and which had been his home for twenty odd years and had been the very heart of the family for four generations of Turners, passed into the hands of strangers. Only the house was sold. His sister, Ellen, built a new house on the old tennis court

PALTERTON HALL

while her sons, Robin and Timothy, continued to run the farm, but it would never be the same place again.

Sadly too, his beloved Doe Lea Valley is not as it was. Now the M1 motorway has been carved through the valley carrying hundreds of vehicles an hour from London to Yorkshire and beyond. Gone too are all the collieries which dominated the valley and the black mountains of slag have been replaced by green fields. Otherwise little has changed and possibly the changes there have been are for the better.

Youngest brother, George, had decided back in 1967, his future did not lie in farming in Derbyshire. With his wife, Peggy, and five children he left his small farm in Langwith to seek a new life in New Zealand.

Dad hinted that he did not enjoy good health following his retirement in 1978. He suffered the first of many heart attacks a year or so later and it seemed that one followed another with increasing regularity after that. They had nothing really to keep them in that part of the world and I lived several hours drive away in Kent. My mother longed to see more of the family but he resisted all suggestions from both of us that they should sell up and move south, preferring in stead to remain in Solihull with the garden he tended with loving care and in which he sat for hour after hour writing the story of this life. The garden was hard work at times and he continued to do too much and it seemed that hardly a year went by without further heart problems and his doctor finally told him the he must give up his garden and find somewhere to live without any stairs to climb if he wanted to prolong his life. So, in the autumn of 1986, he and my mother moved to Rainham in Kent where they found a beautiful flat only fifteen minutes by road from my own home in Sittingbourne.

He had settled in surprisingly well in the new surroundings and enjoyed taking long walks in the countryside when the weather permitted and found some little country pubs where they would go for a ploughman's lunch. He also renewed old friendships particularly with old pals from the Glider Pilot Regiment many of who lived within reasonable travelling distance. My mother loved being close to the family and seeing her grandchildren regularly and I got to know my father better than I had all my life. We would talk for hours particularly on the subject of sport about which we were equally fanatical.

Sadly his health still gave cause for concern although he went for long periods when he felt very well indeed. However regular scares resulted in further stays in hospital. When he spent Christmas Day with us in 1988 he told me he had not felt so well for five years but within forty-eight hours he was back in hospital with another heart attack but unbelievably he was soon home again but only the shadow of the father I had known. I knew this could not go on and that it was only a matter of time before I would get the phone call I dreaded. This finally came just after I had arrived at work – 26 January 1989.

It was a bright and frosty morning, he was waiting to be

collected for a check-up at the hospital when finally his heart could take no more and he died in his own sitting room. My mother, as she had been for 48 years, was at his side supporting him; the most wonderful wife and mother any man could wish for.

Of course I knew a lot of his war stories, I had heard them many times but never realised quite what a part he played until the old Regiment rang and asked if I would mind if they draped the regimental flag over his coffin at the funeral. Mind! It was one of the proudest moments of my life.

The more I have found out about him the prouder of him I have become. I just wish I'd known it all years ago. It would have explained many things. He was a hard Dad but he was brought up hard. His mother didn't even kiss him goodbye when he went off to the war. She just shook his hand and said "Good Afternoon!" No wonder he was not demonstrative himself but it meant we, as boys, never felt really close to him although we always respected him. His mother has a lot to answer for.

As I say, he had much in common with the rest of his family and they were all difficult to get close to and reluctant to reveal their emotions. He was a perfectionist and expected nothing less from others. At any game he was ultra competitive. Even when Alan and I were quite small there was no quarter given. His brothers were the same and I well remember the three of them, by then all in their forties or fifties, playing croquet on the front lawn till dark with none of them prepared to concede defeat and many of the local villagers lined up to watch the spectacle.

As can be seen from the number of pages devoted to it, his Army life was the most important thing he ever did. I think it was because he was allowed to develop away from the influences of his family and become a person in his own right, that he enjoyed it so much. If he had stayed at home he would have been under his mother's influence but I don't believe that would have lasted. Unlike his brother Arthur, he was always destined to do more than just devote himself to the land much as he loved it. As a result of his broadening his horizons, it was always to him that his family turned when they needed advice. I always looked up to him and valued his opinions to the day he died.

He made an instant impact on anyone he met - sometimes good, sometimes quite the opposite. He was loyal to those who supported him and respected loyalty in others. Love him or not, you could never ignore him. I wish I had such a story to tell

His story is more than a personal one, it is a social history of a big part of the twentieth century, of men who survived by sweat and toil and fought for their country in times of war. He was a very private man who, like the rest of his family, rarely showed his true emotions. I only ever saw him close to tears twice. Once he called at my office to tell me of my brother, Alan's death in 1972. The other occasion was many years earlier at Capenor when he brought home the dead body of his beloved Dan, the golden Labrador Retriever we had for only two years in the early 1950s but from whom he was inseparable, who had been knocked down and killed by a lorry close to our home.

Strangely enough, this episode is not mentioned in his story even though it had a profound effect on him at the time. It is however obvious from these pages that he cared much about many things; his love of the land, the plight of the poor in the depression, his childhood holidays at Rock House, his magnificent horse, Captain, the death of his great friend, Tony Brachi. All show a man of great feeling and emotion. It is a shame that he could not let these feeling out more often to those who loved him.

He did not suffer fools gladly or bad workmanship and he admired the skills of craftsmen his motto was, 'If a thing is worth doing, it is worth doing well', a philosophy he followed all his life as scholar, farmer and soldier. In games, in sport, drawing, carpentry and handwriting or anything he set his hand to he always gave nothing less than his best. He had achieved more than many men in a full life but was always modest about his own successes just as he was economical in his praise of others.

If I were to have asked him what he thought of his life I know exactly what the reply would have been – the same as it always was when pleased with something he, or others, had done – "Not bad!" he would say, "Not bad!".

~~~~~~~~~~~~~~~~~~

His wife, my mother, Grace, survived him by eleven years. Although she was very fit and enjoyed good health, vanity stopped her from using a stick to help her on her daily walks and, almost inevitably, she had several falls. The last of these in December 1999 necessitated an operation on her hip and unfortunately she picked up an infection in hospital which turned into septicaemia from which she eventually died in July 2000.

Christopher Turner